THE NATIONAL ASSOCIATION OF
FLOWER ARRANGEMENT SOCIETIES

# ARRANGING
# EVERLASTING
# FLOWERS

A step-by-step guide to creating
spectacular flower arrangements

"Creation, Aspiration,
The Pleasures of Life."

Sir Geoffrey Jellicoe

A design which suggests the art of
illuminated writing. Every minute detail
in the delicate, flowing design is composed
from perfectly prepared and very carefully
handled pressed petals, leaves and tendrils.

The arranger, Pat Kenrick, was inspired by
the words of Sir Geoffrey Jellicoe:
Creation, Aspiration, The Pleasures of Life.

THE NATIONAL ASSOCIATION OF
FLOWER ARRANGEMENT SOCIETIES

# ARRANGING
# EVERLASTING
# FLOWERS

A step-by-step guide to creating
spectacular flower arrangements

Compiled by Mary Newnes

Foreword by
HRH Duchess of York

EBURY PRESS, LONDON

Published by Ebury Press
Division of The National Magazine Company Ltd
Colquhoun House
27–37 Broadwick Street
London W1V 1FR

First impression 1987

ISBN 0 85223 627 1

Editors: Gillian Haslam and Eileen Lloyd
Art Director: Frank Phillips
Designer: Grahame Dudley
Photographer: Di Lewis
Illustrator: Julia Holmes

Filmset by Advanced Filmsetters (Glasgow) Ltd

Printed and bound in Italy by New Interlitho, S.p.a., Milan

Photograph on page 9 by HRH Prince Andrew

# CONTENTS

# INTRODUCTION

The pleasure we find in decorating our homes with flowers need not be restricted to the growing seasons of the year; it can be continued and enjoyed throughout the months when most gardens offer only a limited supply to pick from and when fresh flowers can be very expensive. By the time the early winter arrives, the knowledge-able harvester will have a store of attractive and inspiring bunches and boxes full of contents waiting to be turned into everlasting arrangements.

These enthusiasts will need no encouragement; others may need convincing that the dusty grasses standing on a window sill or sad arrangements, standing forgotten in corners, are of the past. The aim of this book is to suggest ideas to please both the committed and the unconvinced.

With the dry, centrally heated and sometimes air conditioned atmosphere in today's homes everlasting arrangements do have a special place, but it is important that we should not take the word everlasting too literally. With this title goes the message that every arrangement does, indeed, have a limited life. If it is to give pleasure it must be in pristine condition, never faded, dusty, battered or badly assembled. It is not and should not be thought of as an apology for a fresh arrangement—each has its place.

Using some fresh material mixed with everlasting increases the scope for designing arrangements which have a comparatively long life, and the replacement of fresh within a dried framework can be helpful to those whose time is precious. It is interesting, also, to experiment with textures and colours in this way. A number of examples are included in a special section of this book. Both 'Proteas' and 'Art Nouveau' show how a dramatic idea can become a quick-change outline for a few fresh flowers. The 'Hogmanay' arrangement emphasizes the interesting use of contrasting textures. A colour theme has been developed in 'The Midas Touch' within the framework of the preserved leaves.

In the Thanksgiving and Christmas section, the emphasis is some-times on fresh material and sometimes on everlastings and the result is a selection of easy-to-follow ideas for the festive season.

The sizes of the arrangements and the styles and methods used to produce them vary greatly but here are suggestions to suit many settings. Some demand space, not only as finished arrangements but when harvesting and storing all that is included. Others, in complete contrast, are small; little pictures full of charming detail, tiny flowers used in gifts and posies for a bedside table.

Just as in the companion *NAFAS Book of Flower Arranging*, each item of plant material used in the arrangements is named. Shown first is the name by which it is most likely to be found in horticultural reference books and nurserymen's lists. Common names, where they are known, are given last and, in the text, the name by which the plant is most likely to be familiar is used. For instance, statice is used rather than limonium but helichrysum is used instead of strawflower, simply because strawflower can be found for a number of papery-textured annuals. Similarly, holly appears in the text and not ilex, and gypsophila, not baby's breath. It is hoped the detailed lists of plants will mean there is no confusion between flower arrangers the world over.

The arrangements in this book have been created by members of The National Association of Flower Arrangement Societies and they share them with you in the hope that they will give pleasure.

**BUCKINGHAM PALACE**

Flowers have always given me joy and I remember especially those which were arranged for my wedding by members of the National Association of Flower Arrangement Societies.

The idea behind this book is to suggest some new ways in which the love of flowers may be shared with others, and I hope it will give many hours of pleasure to all those who read it.

*Sarah*

# ACKNOWLEDGEMENTS

When The National Association of Flower Arrangement Societies and Ebury Press asked me to compile the content and write the text for this companion book to *The NAFAS Book of Flower Arranging*, we did not know that HRH the Duchess of York would honour the members of the Association by consenting to become the Royal Patron. On behalf of NAFAS and everyone involved in this publication, I offer our gratitude for her message of good wishes and thank her for allowing her photograph to be included.

Once more I have relied on good friends for their help and I am especially pleased to have this opportunity to thank the many members of the Association who allowed their work to go through a selection process. It was rewarding for me, and I hope also for them, to be able to stage an autumn exhibition of more than 100 items and this was held at the church of St Mary-at-Lambeth, the home of the Tradescant Trust. These varied and fascinating exhibits were transported from place to place by post, rail, air or car and finally reached London and the exhibition after being unpacked three times. For their invaluable help in providing posting houses, transport, careful handling and staging expertise I thank my team of Joan Reffell, Betty Treweeke and G. W. Nicholson, and also Dorothy Simcock for the catalogue. At the Tradescant Trust we were given every assistance by Mrs Rosemary Nicholson, her husband and their team of volunteers. The arrangers of twenty-one of these exhibits will find their work included in this book and their names appear alongside.

The other arrangements were photographed in homes, and to all our patient hosts our thanks are due for their welcome and help—Mrs D. Beresford, Mr and Mrs J. Cooke, Mrs J. Fry, Margaret Helman, Judy Bardrick, and Mr Peter de Savary of Littlecote Park. For the photographs taken in the village of Fotheringhay I thank Stephanie Gould of the Castle Farm Guest House and the Vicar and Churchwardens of the Parish Church.

In most cases the flower arrangers travelled long distances, and I wish them to know how much I enjoyed their enthusiasm and their flowers. Their names, too, appear with their arrangements. They will wish to join me in thanking the photographer, Di Lewis, for her skill and her sense of humour, and Kirsty, her assistant, who surely has qualified as a flower-arranging-team supporter.

By thanking all those who have helped me in the preparation of the book, I hope it is apparent how much I have appreciated being invited to compile it. Home tasks have been neglected but there has been no criticism and for this, too, I am grateful.
MARY NEWNES

*Four little Christmas trees decorate a pine corner shelf. They are easily made from a cone of chicken wire packed with wet foam and covered with pieces of spruce. They can be decorated with bows, baubles or larch cones wired into the tree. (Arranger: Vivien Bolton).*

# EVERLASTING
# ARRANGEMENTS

# MOTHER'S DAY

*The posy of everlasting flowers, arranged specially to go with the little cupid candle-holder, makes this a very personal and special gift, feminine in its colouring and in the daintiness of the flowers.*

*1* Place the bowl on its stand and the candlestick on its right. Turn the little cupid half-way towards the bowl and place it slightly to the front. He must be part of the finished design and looking at the flowers. Use eucalyptus first; some of the leaves should be removed to show the tiny buds at the tips, which will give a very light outline, and the leaves left on nearer the middle will make a grey-mauve background for the pink flowers. Keep the effect simple and work to create an 'all-round' arrangement with some stems taken to the back and the sides.

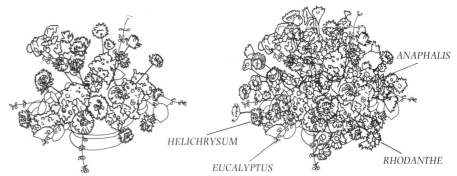

HELICHRYSUM

EUCALYPTUS

ANAPHALIS

RHODANTHE

*2* Follow the same lines with the helichrysum flowers, the smallest buds at the outside, the largest flowers on much shorter stems. Recess some quite close to the foam. Add the anaphalis. The sprays of tiny white flowers again follow the lines of the design, some facing out towards the back, some recessed, some brought forward. This will avoid too perfectly spherical a finish.

*3* Complete the arrangement with the rhodanthe flowers, whose yellow centres are surrounded by deep pink, in some cases fading to almost white at the tips of the petals. They, too, should have their wired stems cut at varying lengths. Arrange them in little groups of about five flowers before adding them to the design.

**SIZE**
25 cm × 29 cm (10 in × 11½ in).

**CONTAINER**
A white china bowl, 15 cm (6 in) in diameter and 5 cm (2 in) high.

**ACCESSORIES**
A carved Chinese stand, 4 cm (1½ in) high. Cupid candlestick and candle, 30½ cm (12 in) high overall.

**EQUIPMENT**
An oblong of dry foam, used on end, anchored by a special sprog fixed with a putty substance to the bowl. The foam stands 5 cm (2 in) above the bowl's rim.

**FOLIAGE**
Glycerined
    *Eucalyptus glaucescens* (Tingiringi gum).

**FLOWERS**
All air dried, the stems wired and then covered with florists' tape
    *Anaphalis yedoensis (A. cinnamonea)* (pearly everlasting).
    *Helichrysum bracteatum* (strawflower, everlasting daisy).
    *Rhodanthe manglesii (Helipterum manglesii)* (Swan River everlasting).

**ARRANGER**
Pauline Mann

# GIFTS

*A plain straw hat decorated with everlasting flowers for a young guest,
perhaps at a summer wedding, and a paperweight with a delicate pressed
flower design. Both are understated and this is their charm.*

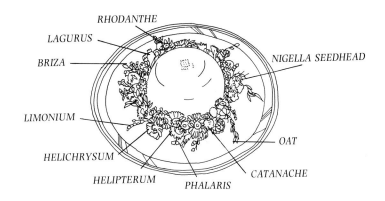

## THE HAT

### SIZE
41 cm (16 in) in diameter; outside diameter of the crown 19 cm (7 in).

### EQUIPMENT
Florist's stub wires and silver reel wire. Needle and thread.

### FLOWERS
Air dried
   *Catanache caerulea* (Cupid's dart, blue succory).
   *Helichrysum bracteatum* (strawflower, everlasting daisy), wired.
   *Helipterum roseum* (*Acroclinium roseum*) (sunray).
   *Limonium latifolium* (broad-leaved sea lavender).
   *Rhodanthe manglesii* (*Helipterum manglesii*) (Swan River everlasting).

### GRASSES
Air dried
   *Avena sativa* (oat).
   *Briza maxima* (greater quaking grass, pearl grass).
   *Lagurus ovatus* (hare's-tail grass, rabbit's-tail grass).
   *Phalaris canariensis* (canary grass).

### SEEDHEADS
Air dried
   *Nigella damascena* (love-in-a-mist).
   *Stachys grandiflora* (*Betonica grandiflora, B. macrantha*) (betony, woundwort).

### ARRANGER
Betty Beswick

*1* The garland for the hat is worked in a strip, approximately 76 cm (30 in) long. Use the wired helichrysum every so often through the design to give strength but all the other material is held in place with the reel wire. This keeps the design light in weight but it does mean care has to be used to avoid snapping off heads from their stems as the wire is taken round them. Start with a small bunch around a helichrysum and then work from that wire stem, the rope of flowers coming towards you. Make sure the finished circlet will lie smoothly round the crown of the hat, with some of the material going out over the brim and some up the crown. When it is completed, trim off any surplus wires and stems and then stitch in place.

## THE PAPERWEIGHT

### SIZE
9 cm (3½ in) in diameter.

### EQUIPMENT
Paperweight blank, supplied with its self-adhesive backing (available by mail order or from craft shops). PVA glue, tweezers, cocktail stick.

### FOLIAGE
Pressed:
   *Acaena* 'Blue Haze' ('Pewter') (New Zealand burr).
   *Geranium robertianum* (herb Robert), the red leaves.

### FLOWERS
Pressed
   *Bellis perennis* (daisy).
   *Myosotis sylvatica* (forget-me-not).
   *Potentilla nepalensis* 'Miss Willmott' (cinquefoil).

### OTHER PLANT MATERIAL
Vine tendrils, pressed.

### ARRANGER
Elsie Franklin

*1* Cut the mount to fit the recess of the paperweight. Work out the design with the daisy and the potentilla in the middle. Use the acaena foliage to give curving lines and add groups of forget-me-not flower heads. Place the vine tendrils around the outside of the design and then some small pieces of the herb Robert; this will pick up the colour of the potentilla.

*2* When you are satisfied with the design, fix everything in place on the mount using a tiny spot of glue on the end of a cocktail stick. Press each piece in place quite firmly.

*3* Turn the paperweight upside-down and lay the mount in the recess. Press the adhesive backing on and make sure it is firm all round the edge. There must not be any movement. Other materials can be used for a mount, felt for instance (this can be used also as a backing).

# GLEANINGS

*An arrangement standing on a hall table where the mirror reflects the leaves and fruits; this emphasizes the variation in textures which can be enjoyed in long-lasting arrangements. The polished rich brown of the glycerined mahonia leaf is very different on its reverse side. Equally interesting is the inclusion of onions and garlic, used with the many different gourds.*

1 Line the container to protect it from damage before putting the wooden block in place. Establish the outline for the design with the feathery Natal grass at the top and a triangle of mahonia leaves from the centre of the foam, the top one following the line of the grass but to its left. Add two long stems of the Chinese lanterns, one up at the back, turned towards the mirror, the other coming out of the foam on the right, low and curving round over the edge and towards the front of the table. The aspidistra leaves follow, two behind the lower stem of Chinese lanterns, one behind the grass, another coming forward at the front. Add a spray of beech leaves on the right, to come in front of the handle.

2 Use the rhododendron leaves between the aspidistra leaves on the right, and turn one to show the paler side. A short stem of Chinese lanterns is added in front of the large leaves. The foxtail grasses go in here also; one of the seedheads curves forward, contrasting against the largest rhododendron leaf, another is just above it. Hang one wired gourd over the rim of the kettle on the left.

3 Add the four cones on the left in a slightly staggered line. Around these group the gourds, mixing the shapes and textures, the largest standing in front of the jam kettle with the onions and garlic. A few gourds may need wire stems but most can be carefully balanced if the cones and the leaves are firmly in place. Tuck in Natal grass between the rhododendron leaves on the right, so that it hangs over the aspidistra leaves and a glycerined hellebore leaf between the aspidistra and the cone at the front.

*SIZE*
86 cm × 71 cm (34 in × 28 in).

*CONTAINER*
A brass jam kettle, 36 cm (14 in) in diameter and 15 cm (6 in) deep.

*EQUIPMENT*
Two blocks of dry foam placed on top of a block of wood. The foam stands 7½ cm (3 in) above the rim of the container and is taped in place from the back to the front.

*FOLIAGE*
Glycerined
  *Aspidistra elatior* (cast-iron plant).
  *Fagus sylvatica* (common beech).
  *Mahonia lomariifolia* 'Charity'.
  *Rhododendron sinograñde.*
  *Helleborus foetidus* (stinking hellebore).

*CONES*
Large pine cones given strong wire stems.

*BERRIES*
*Physalis alkekengi franchetii* (Chinese lantern, bladder cherry), air dried.

*GRASSES*
Air dried
  *Pennisetum orientale* (foxtail millet).
  *Rhynchelytrum repens* (*R. rosea*) (Natal grass, elephant grass).

*OTHER PLANT MATERIAL*
*Cucurbita pepo orifera* vars. (ornamental gourds). Onions and garlic.

*ARRANGER*
G. W. Nicholson

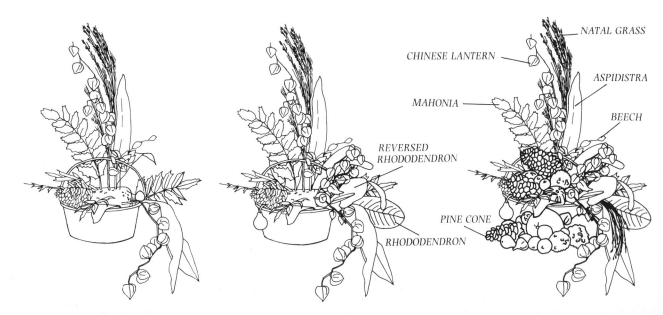

NATAL GRASS

CHINESE LANTERN

ASPIDISTRA

MAHONIA

BEECH

REVERSED
RHODODENDRON

PINE CONE

RHODODENDRON

# NOSTALGIA

*The inspiration for both these designs was found when considering the delights of Victoriana. A collection of early post-cards provided the idea for the one on the left. The one on the right is derived from a renewal of interest in tightly bunched posies, a development from an earlier use of nosegays. Both arrangers chose a rich dark red for the backgrounds and carried this colour through into their designs. Remembering how popular lace was in the 19th century, one uses lace while the other suggests it with pressed flowers.*

## THE PICTURE

### SIZE
Frame, $21\frac{1}{2}$ cm × $25\frac{1}{2}$ cm ($8\frac{1}{2}$ in × 10 in).

### EQUIPMENT
Background composed of shaped cream card pasted over dark red card. Dark wooden frame, glazed and ready for hanging. Scissors, tweezers, nail file, cocktail sticks. Pencil, ruler, soft rubber, magnifying glass.

### FOLIAGE
Pressed
   *Adiantum raddianum (A. cuneatum)* (maidenhair fern).
   *Berberis thunbergii atropurpureum* (purple-leaf barberry).
   *Crataegus monogyna* (hawthorn).
   *Daucus carota* (wild carrot).
   *Hypericum* sp. (St John's wort).
   *Ligustrum ovalifolium* 'Aureum' (golden privet).
   *Senecio jacobaea* (ragwort).
   *Tanacetum parthenium* (feverfew).

### FLOWERS
Pressed
   *Bellis perennis* (daisy).
   *Crataegus monogyna* (hawthorn), buds and flowers.
   *Daucus carota* (wild carrot).
   *Dianthus barbatus* (sweet William).
   *Rumex acetosella* (sheep's sorrel).
   *Sambucus nigra* (European elder), buds and flowers.
   *Saxifraga moschata* (musky saxifrage), buds and flowers.
   *Spiraea × arguta* (bridal wreath, foam of May).
   *Urtica dioica* (stinging nettle).

### ARRANGER
Enid Bradbury

The diagrams show how the design is built up.

### OUTLINING THE CENTRE

### COMPLETING THE CENTRE

Flowers
Saxifrage (flowers).
Hawthorn (flowers).
Daisy (buds).

Foliage
Hawthorn.
Maidenhair fern.

Flowers
Elder (flowers and buds).
Hawthorn (buds).
Saxifrage (buds).
Stinging nettle ('catkins').
Sweet William.
Wild carrot.

Foliage
Berberis
Feverfew
Privet
Ragwort
St John's wort.

### THE CORNERS AND LACE-LIKE BORI

Border flowers
Wild carrot and bridal wreath.

Corner flowers
Sheep's sorrel.
Saxifrage (flowers and buds).
Hawthorn.
Elder (buds).

Corner foliage
Wild carrot.

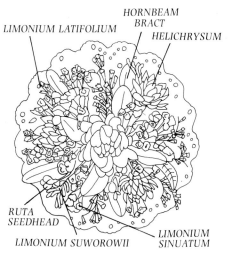

LIMONIUM LATIFOLIUM

HORNBEAM BRACT

HELICHRYSUM

RUTA SEEDHEAD

LIMONIUM SUWOROWII

LIMONIUM SINUATUM

*1* Glue the lace round the edges of the cork discs and cut the foam about $\frac{1}{2}$ cm ($\frac{1}{4}$ in) thick. Glue this to the cork and chamfer it off towards the edges. Divide the prepared plant material into three equal parts.

*2* Glue the flowers, leaves and seedheads to the foam, starting from the outside, over the lace but leaving about $1\frac{1}{2}$ cm ($\frac{1}{2}$ in) showing. Work towards the middle keeping the tight, Victorian posy form. Finish with a well shaped helichrysum in the middle of each posy. For this design do not use the fully opened flowers showing their yellow centres.

*3* Place a loop or a hook at the top of the ribbon and trim the other end neatly. Space the posies evenly, about 18 cm (7 in) apart, the top one with its centre just below the fixing loop.

## THE POSIES

### SIZE
Overall length, with ribbon, 61 cm (24 in); posies 10 cm (4 in) in diameter.

### EQUIPMENT
Three cork discs, $6\frac{1}{4}$ cm ($2\frac{1}{2}$ in) in diameter and $\frac{1}{4}$ cm ($\frac{1}{8}$ in) thick. White lace, 90 cm × 3 cm (36 in × 1 in) (dip this in coffee to give an antique effect). Red velvet ribbon 61 cm × $2\frac{1}{2}$ cm (24 in × 1 in). Small pieces of dry foam. Glue.

### FOLIAGE
Glycerined
   *Carpinus betulus* (hornbeam), the bracts from the fruits.
   *Choisya ternata* (Mexican orange).

### FLOWERS
Air dried
   *Helichrysum bracteatum* (strawflower, everlasting daisy).
   *Limonium sinuatum* (notch-leaf or winged statice).
   *Limonium suworowii* 'Pink Pokers' (Russian or rat's tail statice).
   *Limonium latifolium* (broad-leaved sea lavender).

### SEEDHEADS
*Ruta graveolens* 'Jackman's Blue' (rue).

### ARRANGER
Jennifer Le May

# MEDLEY

*Flowers from various seasons have been preserved and are displayed here in a style which found great favour with the Victorians. The oval dome has been given a new inner base of crimson velvet, a colour which is repeated in the flowers and in the setting.*

*1* Secure the container to the base with a putty substance. Cover the foam with individual petals of hydrangea. Place the gypsophila sprays, the box and the small hellebores to fit the dome and, as you work, make sure this outline is not exceeded.

*2* Take the two larger hellebores and place them in the heart of the design. Then put the small roses near the top and the bottom, and follow with the larger roses. As this arrangement will be enjoyed from all sides, repeat a similar design at the back.

*3* Fill in the spaces with the seedheads and the various kinds of flowers, turning some heads to the sides and the back. Remember to keep the oval shape so that the dome will fit over the finished design comfortably. The list of flowers given above shows great variety, and one of the charms of the design is in finding some on one side and some on the other. The Victorian fan and the little dish of pot-pourri are in keeping with the style of the arrangement.

## SIZE
Base 25 cm (10 in) across, dome 30½ cm (12 in) high.

## CONTAINER
A small tin, 9 cm (3½ in) in diameter, covered in red velvet to match the base.

## EQUIPMENT
Dry foam to fit the tin and standing 3 cm (1½ in) above the rim. Wires. Gutta-percha tape to cover wire stems.

## FOLIAGE
*Buxus sempervirens* (common box), glycerined and bleached by sunlight.
Rose, dried with desiccant granules.

## FLOWERS
Air dried
  *Alchemilla mollis* (lady's mantle).
  Delphinium.
  *Eryngium maritimum* (sea holly).
  *Gypsophila paniculata* 'Bristol Fairy' (chalk plant, baby's breath).
  *Helipterum roseum (Acroclinium roseum)* (sunray).
  *Helleborus foetidus* (stinking hellebore).
  *Hydrangea macrophylla* (common or French hydrangea).
  *Limonium sinuatum* (notch-leaf or winged statice).
  *Limonium suworowii* 'Pink Pokers' (Russian or rat's tail statice).
Dried with desiccant granules (these flowers require wire stems)
  *Convallaria majalis* (lily-of-the-valley).
  *Gentiana septemfida* (gentian).
  *Helleborus orientalis* (Lenten rose).
  Polyanthus.
  Roses, 'Pink Grootendorst' and Garnet rose.
  *Zinnia elegans*.

## SEEDHEADS
Air dried
  *Nigella damascena* (love-in-a-mist).
  *Papaver somniferum* (opium poppy).

## ARRANGER
Joan Cooper

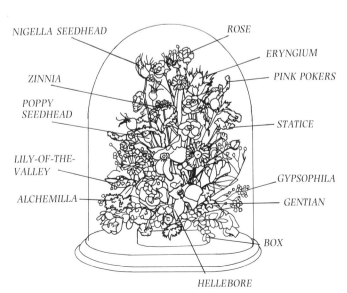

NIGELLA SEEDHEAD

ROSE

ERYNGIUM

PINK POKERS

ZINNIA

POPPY SEEDHEAD

STATICE

LILY-OF-THE-VALLEY

GYPSOPHILA

GENTIAN

ALCHEMILLA

BOX

HELLEBORE

# EVERLASTING
# DAISIES

*A charming posy of dried ferns and flowers decorates a fireplace, no longer in use but an important feature in the hall of this home. The curving shape of the setting is repeated and good use is made of the black background and the glossy black fire front to show off the bright colours.*

*SIZE*
40½ cm × 30½ cm (16 in × 12 in).

*CONTAINER*
None.

*EQUIPMENT*
Two rounds of dry foam covered in thin plastic; one round of dry foam covered in black tissue paper. The three rounds of foam are anchored together with two wires running through them. The black one should be on top. They stand 6½ cm (2½ in) above the fire front when in position.

*FOLIAGE*
Pressed
  Various ferns.

*FLOWERS*
Air dried
  *Achillea filipendulina* (fern-leaved yarrow).
  *Helichrysum bracteatum* (strawflower, everlasting daisy).
  *Lagurus ovatus* (hare's-tail or rabbit's-tail grass).
  *Limonium sinuatum (Statice sinuatum)* (notch-leaf or winged statice).
All the flowers, grasses and ferns are commercially preserved and, in the case of the grasses and some of the ferns, lightly coloured a chrome yellow.

*ARRANGER*
Margaret Newman

*1* Put the foam blocks in place centrally behind the fire front, the top block standing 6½ cm (2½ in) above this. Create the oval outline with flat forms and spikes, the ferns first and then the grasses, these last being used in little tapering bunches rather than singly. To complete the outline, add the flat flowers of the achillea (smaller side heads will be suitable) and a few helichrysums, all in profile. To complete the outline, add a few sprays of the pink statice near the top.

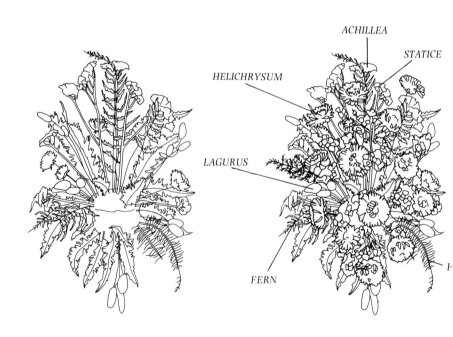

*2* Take the dark purple-blue statice through the middle of the design and add a little more of the pink nearer the outside. In front of these flowers add more ferns and the bright and variously coloured helichrysums, the pink running through the middle. Grade the sizes so that the largest flowers are nearest the centre, but do not lose the mixed-posy appearance and the Victorian effect.

24

# EMILY'S SAMPLER

*A visit to the Victoria and Albert Museum in South Kensington, London, inspired this design. Pressed flowers, leaves, stamens and seedheads are used to interpret the motifs suggested by Bible stories and legends. The inner surround depicts the grapevine with, top centre, the Spies of Canaan returning with the gigantic bunch of grapes. In the centre 'The Tree of Life' is topped with a heart shot through with an arrow and then crowned. Flower motifs were common in old samplers and this border is typical.*

## SIZE
$40\frac{1}{2}$ cm × 28 cm (16 in × 11 in).

## EQUIPMENT
Mounting board covered with several layers of gauze (or other very fine padding material). Silk. Frame with backing board and glass, and fittings for hanging. Stick-glue and paper glue. Fine knitting needle or blunt cocktail stick. Tweezers or nail file. Knife for cutting card.

## PRESSED PLANT MATERIAL
See the diagram.

## ARRANGER
Kathleen Williams

1  *Astrantia major* (masterwort), flower.
2  *Astrantia major*, petals.
3  *Bellis perennis* (daisy), flowers.
4  *Berberis darwinii* (barberry), flowers.
5  Clematis leaves.
6  *Clematis montana* (virgin's bower), leaves.
7  Clematis stems.
8  *Crocosmia × crocosmiflora* var., petals.
9  *Delphinium elatum*, petals.
10 *Dicentra spectabilis* (bleeding-heart) flowers.
11 *Erica carnea (E. herbacea)* (heather heath), florets.
12 *Gazania × hybrida* (treasure flower), petals.
13 *Gazania*, leaves.
14 *Heuchera sanguinea* (coral flower), florets.
15 *Muscaris* sp. (grape hyacinth), flowers.
16 *Passiflora caerulea* (passion-flower), stamens.
17 *Potentilla fruticosa* (cinque flower), flowers.
18 *Santolina chamaecyparissus (S. incana)* (cotton lavender), leaflets.

*1* Select a frame and cut the mounting board and the backing board to fit. Cut the gauze to the size of the mounting board and then the silk $2\frac{1}{2}$ cm (1 in) larger all round. Glue the edges of the mount with the stick glue and turn the edges of the silk over the board firmly to prevent any wrinkles forming on the right side. Mitre the corners and neaten the back with a sheet of cartridge paper.

*2* Place the frame over the mount and work within it. Start with the border. Measure carefully as you make the design so that all the motifs are accurately placed. Work from the top down the sampler and use a nail file or tweezers to pick up each piece of plant material and, with the knitting needle point, apply a tiny blob of paper glue before placing it in position. Look for suitably curving pieces of clematis stems to form the lettering.

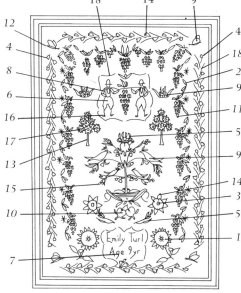

*3* When the design is complete, use a fine paint brush to remove any tiny particles from where they are not wanted. Clean the glass, making sure no finger marks are left, and then assemble: glass first inside the frame, the mount with the design next, and then the backing board. If there is any movement at all, pack out with some more card—the plant material must touch the glass. Exclude the air with parcel packing tape. Do not hang the finished picture in strong sunlight if you wish the colours to remain attractive.

Emily Turl
Age 9yr

# GRASSES

*In this arrangement the colour scheme was chosen to compliment the soft colours in the mirror's frame. The vase repeats these, with just a touch of orange added, and the grasses, of which there is a large selection to pick or to purchase, vary in colour from rich chestnut to soft donkey brown. Brown seed-pods go well with the glycerined brown leaves while the silver-grey reverse of the poplar leaves is repeated by the artemisia and the eryngium.*

*SIZE*
135 cm × 81 cm (53 in × 32 in).

*CONTAINER*
A vase, 36 cm (14 in) high and 20 cm (8 in) across.

*EQUIPMENT*
An inverted cone of dry foam standing 8 cm (3 in) above the rim, taped in place.

*FOLIAGE*
Air dried
   *Crocosmia (Montbretia)* 'Emberglow'.
Glycerined
   *Corylus maxima* 'Purpurea' (purple-leaved filbert, hazel).
   *Dictamnus albus (D. fraxinella)* (dittany, gas plant).
   *Populus alba* (white poplar, abele).

*FLOWERS*
Air dried
   *Artemisia ludoviciana* (white mugwort, white sage, cudweed).
   *Crocosmia (Montbretia)* 'Emberglow'.
   *Eryngium alpinum* (sea holly).
   *Eryngium giganteum* (sea holly).
   *Eryngium planum* (sea holly).

*GRASSES*
Air dried
   *Festuca* sp. (fescue), purchased.
   *Scirpus* sp. (club-rush), purchased.
   *Avena* sp. (oat), purchased.

*SEEDHEADS*
Glycerined
   *Iris graminea* (a Spuria-group iris).
   *Iris siberica* (siberian iris).
Air dried
   *Spiraea japonica.*

*ARRANGER*
Mary Newnes

*1* Place the vase slightly to one side of the mirror and, while working on the design, remember there will be a reflection in it. With some of the tallest fescue grasses establish the height and place shorter stems on the left to give a feathery outline. Add a branch of the poplar and of the hazel leaves to give substance to the centre. Bring short stems of the silver and brown poplar foliage out near the rim of the vase, lower on the right than the left. Add the grey artemisia stems, repeating the outline pattern, and then place some *Eryngium giganteum* with its pale bracts at both sides near the poplar stems.

*2* Following the lines of the first stems of fescue grass, place a few of the montbretia leaves to give slight emphasis to the shape of the design. Next use the spiraea heads in the centre; these will help to mask the foam as well as creating a background for the eryngiums which should be used next. Bring these down through the centre of the arrangement, the larger *E. Alpinum* at the top and in the middle, and the smaller *E. planum* low down. Follow this same line with a few of both kinds of iris pods. Give the sprays of dictamnus leaves false wire stems and then thread this cream colour across from the left down to the right, adding one a little higher in the middle. Next work with two more types of grass, chestnut brown and donkey brown. Use them in groups of one kind, not dotted about but not bunched too closely either. Keep the whole effect light. Used in this way they will give some depth of colour and change of form.

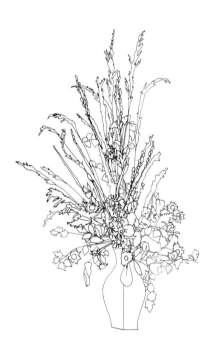

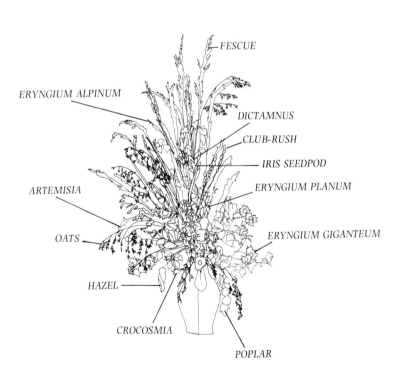

FESCUE

ERYNGIUM ALPINUM

DICTAMNUS

CLUB-RUSH

IRIS SEEDPOD

ERYNGIUM PLANUM

ARTEMISIA

ERYNGIUM GIGANTEUM

OATS

HAZEL

CROCOSMIA

POPLAR

*3* To this arrangement of browns, grey, grey-blue and cream add a touch of orange with the montbretia stems. Finish with the feathery and very pale greenish-cream oats, still following the original line from left to right.

29

SIZE
80 cm × 56 cm (31½ in × 22 in).

CONTAINER
Basket, 40 cm × 25 cm × 8 cm (15¾ in × 10 in × 3½ in).

EQUIPMENT
Shallow plastic dish with an oblong block of dry foam.

FOLIAGE
Glycerined
  *Buxus sempervirens* (box).
  *Fagus sylvaticus* (common beech).
  *Neanthe bella (Chamaedorea elegans)* (parlour palm, dwarf palm, feather palm).

FLOWERS
Air dried
  *Amaranthus hypochondriacus* (prince's feather).
  *Celosia argentea cristata* (cockscomb).
  *Delphinium consolida* (larkspur), blue and pink.
  *Erica cinerea* (bell heather).
  *Helichrysum bracteatum* (strawflower, everlasting daisy).
  *Limonium latifolium* (broad-leaved sea lavender).
  *Limonium sinuatum* (notch-leaf or winged statice).
  *Tanacetum vulgare* (tansy).

CONES
*Larix decidua* (European larch).

SEEDHEADS
Air dried
  *Papaver somniferum* (poppy).

GRASSES
Various spp., dyed, purchased.

ARRANGER
Mary Law

*1* Place the shallow dish with its dry foam centrally along the basket and tape it in place so that it will not move. Form the outline with the grasses, blue larkspur, prince's feather and heather. Next, start to cover the foam by using the glycerined palm leaves and bring one out over the edge of the basket at the front.

*2* Fill in the design with all the other flowers, except the celosias, and add the beech and box foliage. Do not go beyond the original outline, and make sure there is plenty of variation in the lengths of the stems.

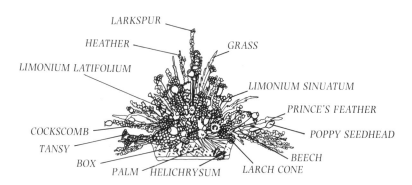

*3* Next add the cones, quite near the centre of the design. Then the poppy heads, with their soft grey colour and less fussy form, should be used throughout the arrangement to give contrast. Add the celosias in the heart of the design; they will link in colour with the brightest of the helichrysums. This same design can be developed into one to be enjoyed from all round, standing on a low table in the middle of a room, for instance. To achieve this, start the design from the middle of the block of foam rather than from two thirds back. It will be necessary to make sure that the arrangement does not become over-crowded and the outline lost as more material is added. Rather less than double the amount of flowers, leaves, grasses and seedheads will be needed.

# COLOUR IMPACT

*A rich assortment of colours in a pale wicker basket is effective against this background. Arranged from a collection of home grown and purchased material, these flowers, grasses and seedheads have been mixed together with the emphasis on colours which look well with dark wood. The basket was chosen for the same reason and, in addition, its style is in harmony with the scale of everything in the arrangement.*

# JACOBEAN

*The inspiration for this interpretation of an embroidered bell-pull came from
a book of needlework illustrations owned since schooldays, coupled with a
lasting fascination for the imaginative flowers and leaves found in the work of
embroideresses of the Jacobean period.*

### SIZE
1 metre (39½ in) long, without the tassel,
12 cm (4¾ in) wide.

### EQUIPMENT
Hardboard (stiff card will do), 99 cm ×
11½ cm (39 in × 4½ in). Dowelling, ¾ cm in
diameter, 30½ cm long (¼ in × 10 in). Linen or
curtain lining, 102 cm × 25½ cm (40 in ×
10 in), plus three small pieces for covering
dowelling. Four wooden beads, ¾ cm (¼ in) in
diameter. A silk tassel. Glue.

### FLOWERS
Air dried
*Lavandula spica* (lavender).
*Limonium sinuatum (Statice sinuatum)*
(notch-leaf or winged statice).

### SEEDHEADS
Air dried
*Papaver somniferum* (opium poppy),
seedhead caps only.
Glycerined
*Rumex obtusifolius* (broad-leafed dock).

### SEEDS
Air dried
*Alstroemeria aurantiaca* (Peruvian lily).
*Althaea rosea* (hollyhock).
*Brassica napus* (rape or cole).
*Calendula officinalis* (pot marigold).
*Cosmos bipinnatus.*
*Eranthis hyemalis* (winter aconite).
*Eryngium maritimum* (sea holly).
*Fritillaria imperialis* (crown imperial).
*Lathyrus odoratus* (sweet pea).
*Lunaria annua (L. biennis)* (honesty,
money plant, moonwort, satin flower).
Millet.
Mustard.
*Myrrhis odorata* (sweet Cicely).
*Phleum pratense* (Timothy grass).
Pumpkin.
Rice (brown).
*Tragopogon pratensis* (Jack-go-to-bed-at-
noon, goatsbeard).
*Trigonella foenum-graecum* (fenugreek).

### STEMS AND GRASS
Bleached and dyed
'Glixia', purchased.

Rye grass (purchased under a variety of
names such as 'temex' and
'ampledermis').

### OTHER PLANT MATERIAL
*Lathyrus odoratus* (sweet pea), tendrils,
pressed.

### ARRANGER
Joan Carver

ALSTROEMERIA SEED
FRITILLARIA SEED
MARIGOLD SEED

STATICE

GLIXIA STEMS }
MUSTARD SEED }

SWEET CICELY SEEDS

FENUGREEK SEEDS }
RAPE SEEDS
GLIXIA STEMS }

SWEET PEA SEED

ERANTHIS SEEDS }
RYE GRASS SPIKELETS }

RYE GRASS SPIKELETS

MILLET

LAVENDER

TOP OF POPPY
SEEDHEAD

PUMPKIN SEED
MARIGOLD SEED
GOATSBEARD SEEDS

MARIGOLD SEEDS
SWEET CICELY SEED
RAPE SEEDS

RYE GRASS SPIKELETS

ERYNGIUM
MARITIMUM SEEDS

GOATSBEARD SEEDS

TIMOTHY GRASS

HOLLYHOCK SEEDS
ALSTROEMERIA SEEDS
GLYCERINED DOCK

MILLET

COSMOS SEEDS }
HONESTY SEEDS }

BEAD

DOWELLING

BROWN RICE
SWEET CICELY SEEDS
MUSTARD SEEDS

SWEET PEA TENDRILS

TASSEL

**1** Machine together the two longer sides of the material, which has
been reinforced with the iron-on stiffening, to form a tube. Press
the seam open and, with the seam at the centre back, mitre the lower
edge and trim close to the stitches. Turn right side out and press flat.
Shape the board to fit and slip inside. Turn in the upper edge and stitch
or glue it securely. Fix a hanging loop at the back, 4 cm (1½ in) from
the top.

**2** Collect all the plant material and put each kind into a separate
container which will be easy to work from. Draw the design on a
piece of tracing or greaseproof paper. Rub the reverse side of this with
a soft (6B) pencil. Lay the paper, reverse side down, on the prepared
base and trace over the design with a hard black (HB) pencil. Remove
the paper.

**3** Glue the chosen seeds, flower heads and tendrils in place. It is
very important to follow the shape of each leaf and flower petal
when placing them in position; a pair of pointed tweezers may help.
Finally, cover three pieces of dowelling with linen and secure them to
the top and bottom edges, add a wooden bead at the outer ends of the
dowelling and the silk tassel in the middle.

# ONE OF A PAIR

*This wall plaque has been designed to be used in any one of three ways. As shown here, it can be hung on its own, or it can be hung with a partner in a similar position. The third option is to join them together lengthways to make a dramatic decoration which is suitable for a flower festival in a church or any other spacious setting. The black background shows off the paler colours beautifully, especially the curves of bleached grass which form an important part of the design.*

## SIZE
91 cm × 18 cm (36 in × 7 in).

## EQUIPMENT
Pegboard covered with finely textured, black, linen-type fabric. Glue.

## FLOWERS
*Echinops ritro* (globe thistle), immature flowers, air dried.

## FOLIAGE
Glycerined
  *Choisya ternata* (Mexican orange).
  *Cupressocyparis leylandii* (leyland cypress).
  *Eucalyptus gunnii* (gum tree).

## SEEDHEADS
Grass, dried and bleached (purchased).
Air dried
  *Dictamnus fraxinella (D. albus)* (dittany, gas plant, burning bush).
  *Dipsacus fullonum* (teasel), burnt.
  *Fagus sylvatica* (common beech).
  *Fritillaria imperialis* (crown imperial).
  Iris.
  *Molucella laevis* (bell's of Ireland).
  *Nigella damascena* (love-in-a-mist).
  *Papaver somniferum* (opium poppy).

## CONES
*Larix decidua* (European larch).
*Pinus sylvestris* (Scots pine).

## ARRANGER
Hilda Buckle

*1* Prepare the background by smoothing the fabric over the pegboard and gluing at the back. Keep the line of the linen threads running straight down and straight across the backing. Mitre the corners and make sure no wrinkles are left on the front. Fix a wire for hanging 10 cm (4 in) down from the top. If a pair is to be made, and these are to be joined together for one long plaque, make a second fixing 10 cm (4 in) up from the bottom on the higher one of the two so that they can be wired together before hanging.

*2* Form the outline of the design with the choisya leaves at the top and then put the curved grass heads in position followed by the eucalyptus leaves and the sprays of cypress.

*3* Continue to build up the design, making sure that the blue echinops and black teasels come down through the design evenly among the many shades of browns and creams. The important 'flowers' just below the middle of the design are made from the split seedheads of the crown imperials. Take care to use some of the plant material so that it will just overlap and so link with the second plaque if two are to be used together.

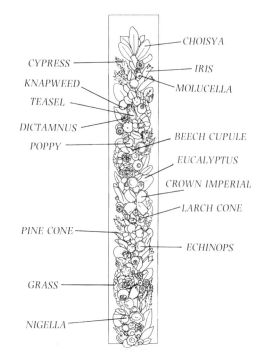

CHOISYA
CYPRESS
IRIS
MOLUCELLA
KNAPWEED
TEASEL
DICTAMNUS
POPPY
BEECH CUPULE
EUCALYPTUS
CROWN IMPERIAL
LARCH CONE
PINE CONE
ECHINOPS
GRASS
NIGELLA

# WINTER EVENING

*All the colours in the comport, with its two figures apparently meeting on the way to market, are found in this arrangement of everlastings. Picked up, too, is the colour of the table. The red velvet curtains make a rich background against which the many shapes and shades can be enjoyed.*

*SIZE*
107 cm × 84 cm (42 in × 33 in).

*CONTAINER*
Antique comport, 43 cm (17 in) high and 33 cm (13 in) across the top.

*EQUIPMENT*
Pinholder with a block of dry foam on top, tied in place with soft string.

*FOLIAGE*
Glycerined
  *Elaeagnus macrophylla* (oleaster), leaves wired and formed into sprays.

*FLOWERS*
Air dried
  *Achillea filipendulina (A. eupatorium)* (fern-leaved yarrow), most sprayed saffron yellow.
  *Amaranthus hypochondriacus* 'Green Thumb' (prince's feather, green variety).
  *Carthamus tinctorius* (safflower, saffron thistle, dyer's saffron).
  *Delphinium consolida* (larkspur).
  *Helichrysum bracteatum* (strawflower, everlasting daisy).
  *Hydrangea macrophylla (H. hortensia, H. opuloides)* (common or French hydrangea).
  *Limonium latifolium* (broad-leaved statice, sea lavender).
  *Limonium sinuatum* (notch-leaf or winged statice).
  *Xeranthemum annuum* (immortelle).

*GRASSES*
Air dried
  Florist's varieties, spray-dyed green, pinkish-purple and deep orange, purchased.

*SEEDHEADS*
Air dried
  *Lunaria annua (L. biennis)* (honesty, money plant, moonwort, satin flower), some pods stripped of their cases.
  *Nigella damascena* (love-in-a-mist).
  *Papaver somniferum* (opium poppy).
  *Stachys lanata (S. byzantina, S. olympica)* (lamb's tongue, lamb's ear, woolly betony).

*ARRANGER*
Joan Dunne

*1* First place five stems of elaeagnus leaves; put one low on the left, a second diagonally across on the right and a little higher, one almost centrally and stems four and five on either side of it, taking these back a little. In front of the lower right-hand stem put in a stem of cream molucella; add more above but nearer the centre and then three more, one by each of the top sprays of elaeagnus. In the middle of the design place another short piece of elaeagnus and add two short stems of molucella, one just behind this spray of leaves and one out to the left. Place a few stems of white larkspur around the design to give finer points. Then add two stems of safflower low on the left and two more nearer the top.

*2* Start to fill in the design with the green spikes of amaranthus, then the flat head of the achillea, the pale ones low to the right of the middle of the design. Add the sea lavender low down near the centre and towards the left. Keep everything within the original outline as you continue. Place the purple and green honesty pods on the left and bring more, this time the silvery inner pods, through into the sea lavender. Add some more of the safflower low on the right but out towards the back. Add two hydrangea heads, one over the edge of the dish on the left and the other quite high in the middle, and the design is ready for the final stages—but remember to take some flowers out from the back of the container for balance and to make it interesting when seen from the sides.

*3* Arrange the grasses into attractive bunches and wire them together. Then put them in place, green on the right, deep orange on the left and pinkish-purple in the middle. Carry this purple colour up with a cluster of the love-in-a-mist seedpods just above and then with the brighter purple-pink xeranthemum flowers bunched in the same way as the grasses. Use the latter near the outline of the arrangement. Add a few finishing touches—two stems of love-in-a-mist seedpods just giving a slightly lighter look to the very top, some white statice flowers in a group by the honesty, a very few poppy seedheads and cream helichrysum flowers and a spray of the silvery honesty tucked in by the central bunch of grasses.

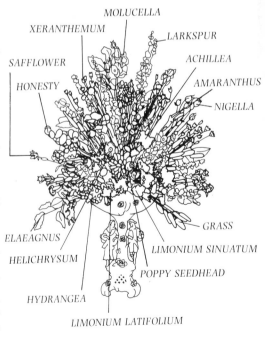

# GARDEN HARVEST

*A stone wall and brown quarry tiles near a garden door provide a setting for
an informal arrangement of many different kinds of easily grown and
harvested seedheads, leaves, and a few flowers. The colours are soft and
natural but have as many subtle variations as the stones in the background.*

## SIZE
145 cm × 107 cm (57 in × 42 in).

## CONTAINER
Two-tier garden bottle carrier, 46 cm (18 in)
high and inside diameter 27 cm (10½ in).

## EQUIPMENT
Two heavy pinholders. Two oblong blocks of
dry foam, 23 cm × 10 cm × 9 cm (9 in ×
4 in × 3½ in).

## FOLIAGE
Pressed
  *Crocosmia (Montbretia)* 'Emberglow'.
  *Polystichum setiferum* (soft shield or hedge
  fern).
Glycerined
  *Quercus robur* (English oak).

## FLOWERS
Air dried
  *Achillea taygetea* (yarrow).
  *Hydrangea macrophylla*
  (*H. hortensis, H. opuloides*) 'Mme. E.
  Mouillière' (common or French
  hydrangea).

## SEEDHEADS
Air dried
  *Allium porrum* (leek).
  *Allium siculum (Nectaroscordum siculum)*.
  *Angelica archangelica*.
  *Delphinium elatum*, hydrid.
  *Molucella laevis* (bells of Ireland).
  *Polemonium caeruleum* (Jacob's ladder,
  Greek valerian).
  *Stachys lanata (S. byzantina, S. olympica)*
  (lamb's tongue, lamb's ear, woolly
  betony).
Glycerined
  *Digitalis purpurea* (common foxglove).
  *Molucella laevis* (bells of Ireland).

## CONES
*Picea* sp. (spruce fir).
*Sciadopitys verticillata* (Japanese umbrella
pine).

## ARRANGER
Mary Newnes

1 With a tall arrangement in a light basket container it is
necessary to add weight at the very back. For this one of the
pinholders is suitable. Put the foam on the pinholders, across the top
tier of the basket, and then tape the blocks securely to the basket.
About 5 cm (2 in) of the foam will stand above the edge if the blocks
are turned on their sides. The delphinium seedheads give the height,
and the oak on the left and the ferns on the right give the width. Put
these in place first and then follow with the molucella, the darker
cream, glycerined stems on the outside and the paler (and more
brittle) dried ones in the middle. Add another longer stem of the oak
towards the back behind the delphiniums; this will give depth of
colour and its weight will give stability to the arrangement.

2 Keeping within this framework add the pale yellow achillea
flowers on both sides, then foxglove seedheads quite high on the
left and a large angelica seedhead over the front of the basket in the
middle. Take both the Jacob's ladder and the *Allium siculum* seedheads
and place these on both sides, with shorter stems nearer the middle.
The pressed leaves of the crocosmia come next; their plainness will act
as a foil for other shapes and they should be placed so that they
accentuate the lines of the arrangement.

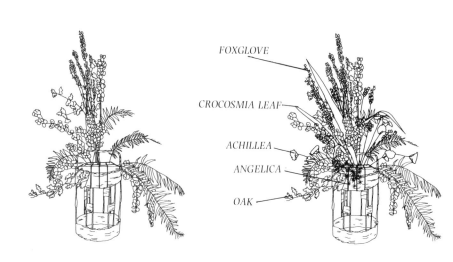

FOXGLOVE

CROCOSMIA LEAF

ACHILLEA

ANGELICA

OAK

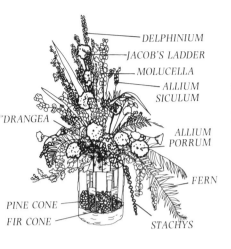

DELPHINIUM
JACOB'S LADDER
MOLUCELLA
ALLIUM
SICULUM

'DRANGEA

ALLIUM
PORRUM

FERN

PINE CONE
FIR CONE

STACHYS

*3* To the browns and soft greens add some grey. First place pieces of the stachys on either side and then take some to the back to contrast in colour and texture with the glycerined oak; this will be seen from the side. More grey is added with the leek seedheads. These vary in density and colour according to when they were picked. Bring them down through the arrangement and add one out to the left and two to the right. Tuck in the pale green hydrangea by the angelica; the bracts of this white variety turn a lovely pale green. Add a few large cones in the lower tier of the basket.

# MAKING PATTERNS

*Aromatic spices, dried seedheads and flowers spiral round a cone to make this tree. The emphasis is on shapes and textures and these are used to form the pattern. The little tree stands in a circle of similar seedheads and flowers but these have been arranged in a less formal way, so that the circle becomes a foil for the tree rather than overstating the idea.*

*1* First fill the flower pot to within $2\frac{1}{2}$ cm (1 in) of the top with a stiff cement mix. Place the cane in the middle. It is essential to get this central and upright. Before the mix sets, place short stems of the paler achillea and alchemilla in it to mask the whiteness. When starting work on the cone it will help to place it on another slim piece of cane so that it can be held easily. Do not press this in too far as the finished cone must sit securely on its stem.

*2* Plan the spiral design by making the start of two curves of the achillea exactly opposite from each other. Use pieces which diminish in size until the two spiralling lines have reached to within 2 cm ($\frac{3}{4}$ in) of the top but have only gone round the cone once. They should be checked to make sure that they are equidistant from each other all the way up. Now take the nigella seedheads and put two lines, graduating the sizes, below the two lines of achillea and follow with spice picks above. Next add two lines of eryngium heads. Complete the covering of the cone with three more lines, the first of spiky heads of sea lavender, next a line of the Jacob's ladder and finally another line of the spice picks. Only the very top will remain uncovered and it should be finished with tiny pieces of achillea, a very small nigella head and a little of the Jacob's ladder.

*SIZE*
Cone: 48 cm × 20 cm (19 in × 8 in).
Circle: 33 cm (13 in) in diameter, $6\frac{1}{2}$ cm ($2\frac{3}{4}$ in) high.

*EQUIPMENT*
A plastic flower pot, 9 cm ($3\frac{1}{2}$ in) size.
A slim cane, $\frac{1}{2}$ cm ($\frac{1}{4}$ in) in diameter, 30 cm (12 in) long. A cone of dry foam, $25\frac{1}{2}$ cm (10 in) tall and 9 cm ($3\frac{1}{2}$ in) in diameter. A circle of dry foam, 18 cm (7 in) in diameter (outside), 10 cm (4 in) in diameter (inside) and 4 cm ($1\frac{1}{2}$ in) deep. A cement-type substance. Bronze-colour ribbon, 36 cm (14 in) long and 5 cm (2 in) wide.

*FLOWERS*
Air dried
   Achillea filipendulina (A. eupatorium) (fern-leaved yarrow).
   Achillea taygetea (yarrow).
   Alchemilla mollis (lady's mantle).
   Eryngium amethystinum (sea holly).
   Helichrysum bracteatum (strawflower, everlasting daisy).
   Limonium latifolium (broad-leaved statice, sea-lavender).
   Nigella damascena (love-in-a-mist).

*SEEDHEADS*
Air dried
   Polemonium caeruleum (Jacob's ladder).
   Spiraea japonica.

*GRASS*
Dried
   Phalaris arundinacea (reed canary grass).

*ACCESSORIES*
A brass tray, 34 cm ($13\frac{1}{2}$ in) in diameter.
Spice picks, purchased, approximately 80.
Small cones or Christmas baubles could be used.

*ARRANGER*
Mary Newnes

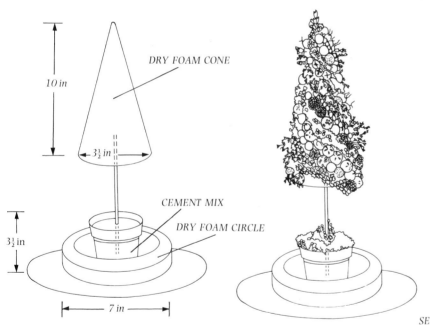

DRY FOAM CONE

10 in

$3\frac{1}{2}$ in

CEMENT MIX

DRY FOAM CIRCLE

$3\frac{1}{2}$ in

7 in

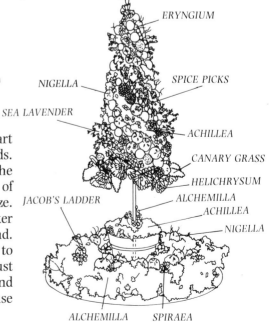

JACOB'S LADDER

ERYNGIUM

NIGELLA

SPICE PICKS

SEA LAVENDER

ACHILLEA

CANARY GRASS

HELICHRYSUM

JACOB'S LADDER

ALCHEMILLA

ACHILLEA

NIGELLA

ALCHEMILLA     SPIRAEA

*3* Leaving room for the flower pot to stand in the middle, start covering the circle, first at the inner edge with eryngium heads. Follow with a circle of achillea, this time interspersing a few of the darker *A. filipendulina*, then add a ring of nigella heads with clusters of Jacob's ladder among them. Try to keep the seedheads even in size. The next circle is of Jacob's ladder but this time mixed with the darker spiraea. Finish covering the circle with feathery alchemilla all round. As you work, the material should curve over the circle and down to table level. When it is finished the foam should be hidden, with just enough space left for the flower pot with its covering of ribbon to stand in the middle. Place the cone on top of the cane and, at its base, use the grasses and wired helichrysum to mask the foam edge.

# INSPIRED BY A
# FAN

*There are six tiny arrangements within this one design and the careful study of a Spanish fan was the inspiration for this detailed work. The many pieces of pressed plants provide enough variety to suggest the delicacy of lace round the edge of the fan and the richness of the decoration in the six panels, each one quite different from the others.*

*SIZE*
36 cm × 27 cm (14 in × 10½ in), including the frame.

*EQUIPMENT*
Glue, latex-type. Pencil, ruler and soft rubber. Scissors, tweezers, nail file and cocktail stick (toothpick). Magnifying glass. Lightweight dark cream card for the fan shape. Dark brown paper for the background.

*PLANT MATERIAL*
All the plant material is pressed and is shown with the diagrams.

*ARRANGER*
Enid Bradbury

42

## PANELS FROM LEFT TO RIGHT—

### 1 FLOWERS
*Rumex obtusifolius* (broad-leafed dock).
*Epilobium hirsutum* (willowherb).

#### FOLIAGE
Grass.
*Trifolium repens* (white or Dutch clover).
*Fumaria officinalis* (common fumitory).

#### SEEDHEADS
*Geranium* (cranesbill).

### 2 FLOWERS
*Chrysanthemum parthenium (Tanacetum parthenium)* (feverfew).
*Sambucus nigra* (elder).
*Polygonum* (knotweed).

#### FOLIAGE
Bracken.
*Sambucus nigra* (elder).

#### SEEDHEADS
*Geranium* (cranesbill).

### 3 FLOWERS
*Crocosmia* sp. *(Monbretia, Tritonia)*
*Viola* sp.
*Stellaria holostea* (greater stitchwort).

#### FOLIAGE
*Chrysanthemum parthenium (Tanacetum parthenium)* (feverfew).
Grass blades.

### 4 FLOWERS
*Melilotus alba* (white melilot).
*Ranunculus ficaria* (lesser celandine).
*Hippocrepis comoso* (horseshoe vetch).
*Convallaria majalis* (lily-of-the-valley).

#### FOLIAGE
Grass blades. Rose.

### 5 FLOWERS
*Astrantia carniolica* 'Rubra' (masterwort).
*Erica carnea (E. herbacea)* (heath, heather).
*Stellaria holostea* (greater stitchwort).

#### FOLIAGE
*Polygonum* (knotweed). Bracken.

#### SEEDHEADS
*Geranium* (cranesbill).

### 6 FLOWERS
*Trifolium repens* (white or Dutch clover).
*Syringa* (lilac).
*Sambucus nigra* (elder).

#### FOLIAGE
*Fumaria officinalis* (common fumitory).
*Chrysanthemum parthenium (Tanacetum parthenium)* (feverfew).

### LOWER HALF CIRCLE

#### FLOWERS
*Daucus carota* (wild carrot).
*Crataegus monogyna* (hawthorn).

### OUTER EDGE

#### FLOWERS
*Daucus carota* (wild carrot).
*Crataegus monogyna* (hawthorn).

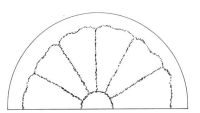

*1* Cut two fan shapes from the cream card and mark them out in sections as shown in diagram 2. Use one card for planning the design and, when this is satisfactory, transfer it to the other card, carefully gluing each piece in place with a tiny drop of glue on the cocktail stick. Each piece can be handled with tweezers or the nail file. Start by covering the pencilled section lines, the scalloped top line and the lower half-circle with wild grass spikelets.

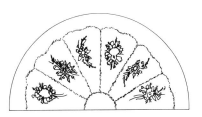

*2* Add the six miniature flower arrangements inside the panels. Take care to avoid damaging any part of the design as you work.

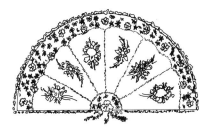

*3* Continue by working on the outer border and the half-circle at the bottom of the fan. For these use the wild carrot, the hawthorn blossom and the white melilot. Keep the design light and dainty. Complete the fan by mounting it on the brown paper which has been cut to fit the frame. Add the suggestion of short ribbons and, for these, use more of the melilot. Make sure the backing to the frame fits firmly and then seal to exclude the air.

# THE LECTERN

*On this handsome brass lectern the marker for the Bible sits across the slight curve of the eagle's wing and the design, although composed of many small items, has a clear pattern, suggesting rich and skilful ecclesiastical embroidery. The setting is the parish church at Fotheringhay, the village where Mary, Queen of Scots was finally imprisoned and where she died in 1587.*

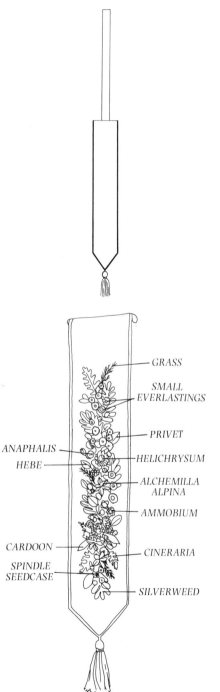

GRASS

SMALL
EVERLASTINGS

PRIVET

ANAPHALIS

HELICHRYSUM

HEBE

ALCHEMILLA
ALPINA

AMMOBIUM

CARDOON

CINERARIA

SPINDLE
SEEDCASE

SILVERWEED

## SIZE
Design 38 cm (15 in), on a corded silk background 76 cm × 10 cm (30 in × 4 in).

## EQUIPMENT
Deep cream corded silk, enough to use double, 155 cm (62 in). Iron-on stiffener 76 cm × 7½ cm (30 in × 3½ in). Additional length of silk or similar material 58 cm × 4 cm (23 in × 1½ in). Gold braid, 1½ cm (½ in) wide. Gold tassel, hand-made from fancy silk and gold-thread 'twist' purchased from needlework supplier. Gum, cocktail stick, nail-varnish remover, tweezers.

## ARRANGER
Hilda Buckle

## FOLIAGE
Pressed
  *Alchemilla alpina* (alpine lady's mantle).
  *Cineraria maritima* (silver-leaved cineraria, dusty miller).
  *Potentilla anserina* (silverweed).
Glycerined
  *Hebe pinguifolia* 'Pagei' (shrubby veronica).
  *Ligustrum ovalifolium* (privet), small leaves.

## FLOWERS
Dried
  *Acanthus mollis* (bear's breeches), stamens.
  *Ammobium alatum* (sandflower, winged everlasting), and *Anaphalis triplinervis* (pearly everlasting), both dyed with hot water dye and re-dried.
  *Cynara cardunculus* (cardoon), petals only.
  *Helichrysum bracteatum* (strawflower, everlasting daisy), small, picked in the bud, opened in airing cupboard.
  Star-flower, tiny everlastings, purchased.

## GRASS
Air dried
  *Alopecurus myosuroides* (slender foxtail), dyed with hot water dye and re-dried.

## SEEDS
Air dried
  *Dictamnus albus* (*D. fraxinella*) (dittany, gas plant).
  *Euonymus europaeus* (spindle-tree).

## SEEDHEADS
Air dried
  *Euonymus europaeus* (spindle-tree).
  *Papaver somniferum* (opium poppy), seedhead caps only.

1 To make the marker, fold the corded silk lengthways and interline it with the stiffener, ironing to the front half. Stitch the sides together. Carefully mitre one end by turning back the corners and lightly stitching in place. Sew the narrow strip of ribbon to the wider piece. This is designed to go under the Bible and inside the back cover, the weight of the pages will then hold the marker in place. Edge the marker with the braid, sewing it on as if it were bias-binding. Sew the tassel in place. Before adding the plant material, work out the design very carefully. Mark the position of the top and bottom on the marker and turn it horizontally across the table. This avoids damaging the fragile material as you work. Have the gum and cocktail stick ready and also the nail-varnish remover in case it is necessary to take off any tiny drops of the gum from the silk.

2 First work at both ends with the loops of grass and then move to the centre and work outwards. Position each piece carefully and remember colour-blending, size and texture. Use the bolder and deeper coloured flowers near the centre and make sure interesting and unusual shapes are glued where they show against the silk.

# THE WRITING
# DESK

*Purple, crimson and gold—these colours were suggested by the travelling
writing desk. It is not possible for everyone to harvest everlastings and here is
an arrangement of flowers and foliage chosen in a garden centre. The soft
finish of the container is interesting when combined with these colours.*

SIZE
69 cm × 58½ cm (27 in × 23 in).

CONTAINER
A gilded brass night-light holder with
pierced cover, 24 cm (9½ in) high and 19 cm
(7½ in) in diameter, the opening 7½ cm (3 in)
across.

EQUIPMENT
A round of dry foam standing 5 cm (2 in)
above the container rim, taped in place.

FOLIAGE
*Fagus sylvatica* (European beech), dyed to
resemble copper beech (commercially
treated).
Fresh
   *Thuja occidentalis* 'Rheingold' (American
   arbor-vitae), three small sprays.

FLOWERS
Air dried
   *Amaranthus hypochondriacus* (prince's
   feather).
   *Limonium sinuatum* (notch-leaf or winged
   statice).
   *Gypsophila paniculata* (baby's breath, chalk
   plant), dyed red.

SEEDHEADS
Air dried
   *Melaleuca* sp. (honey myrtle).

ARRANGER
Mary Newnes

*1* With just three sprays of beech leaves, create an asymmetrical
triangle: one stem on the right, low and forward a little, another
higher on the left and a little shorter, and the third one slightly back
and over to the left at the top. Start to mask the foam and add a touch
of clear green with the short sprays of thuja. Add the stems of
amaranthus, taller at the centre than the beech. Vary the lengths of
these stems, bringing some forwards and taking some back, to avoid
a flat and too fan-like shape.

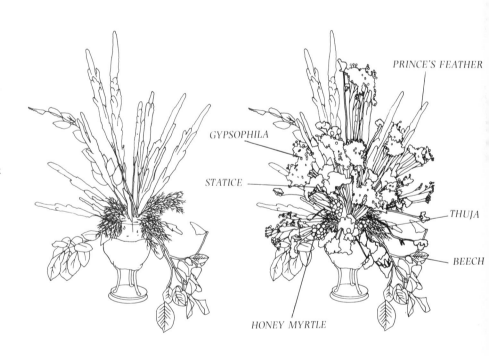

*2* Start to fill in the design with the bright blue statice, continuing
to vary the lengths of the stems and accentuating the original
lines of the beech and the tallest of the amaranthus. Place the stems of
the honey myrtle near the middle. These will give a contrasting shape
as well as adding an interesting touch of pale grey. Finally, add
lightness of texture and brightness of colour with the sprays of red
gypsophila. Do not bring this out beyond the outline but use the lacy
flowers throughout the design, especially to soften the effect of the stiff
statice stems.

## SIZE
29 cm × 23 cm (11½ in × 9 in), frame included.

## EQUIPMENT
Frame with glass. Mounting board, cut to fit (a colour should be selected which will show the chosen flowers to advantage). PVA glue, tweezers and cocktail stick.
All the plant material is pressed.

## FOLIAGE
*Acaena* 'Blue Haze' ('Pewter') (New Zealand burr).

*Geranium robertianum* (herb Robert), red and green.
*Hedera helix* (ivy).
*Potentilla reptans* (cinquefoil).

## FLOWERS
*Alyssum saxatile* (yellow alyssum, gold dust).
*Brachycome iberidifolia* (Swan River daisy).
*Dianthus chinensis* (Indian, Chinese or rainbow pink).
*Iberis* sp.
*Lobelia erinus* (edging lobelia).
*Mina lobata (Quamoclit lobata)* (crimson star glory).

*Myosotis sylvatica* (forget-me-not).
*Papaver rhoeas* (field poppy), buds.
*Phacelia campanularia* (Californian bluebell).
*Ranunculus repens* (creeping buttercup).

## GRASSES
*Briza media* (common quaking grass).
*Luzula campestris* (field woodrush, Good Friday grass, sweep's brush).
*Nardus stricta* (mat grass).
Various curved and straight stalks.

## ARRANGER
Elsie Franklin

# A SUMMER
# BORDER

*This picture suggests a perfectly tended border in a cottage garden. The delicacy and the clear colours of the pressed flowers are shown to great advantage when they are arranged on slender stems. The carved Victorian frame is unusual too; it adds a sense of permanence and balance to the finished picture.*

*1* Plan the design on a matching piece of card and when you are pleased with the result transfer each piece of material to the mount, fixing it in place with a tiny spot of glue from the end of the cocktail stick. For this border design you will need stems of different lengths and, to avoid a static look, it helps to have some which are not completely straight. Place the tallest flowers across the mount first. Next start filling in with shorter pieces and with foliage and grasses. Use a variety of textures and shapes.

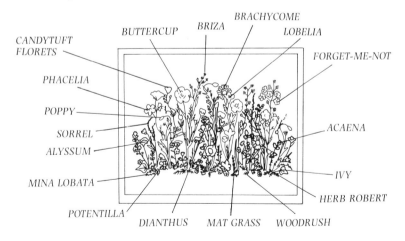

*2* Complete the border with forget-me-not heads and the quaking grass until it looks interesting but not over full. You should be able to look at the picture without seeing everything at once, but it must not become confused. Finish the design with herb Robert and ivy leaves at the bottom. This gives a little weight to the finished picture and prevents a stalky appearance. Put the finished picture in its frame, making sure it fits tightly and that air is excluded.

# SATIN FLOWERS

*Here, in a bathroom, standing on a marble-topped cabinet, the arrangement picks up the colours all around it. The jar, filled with everlasting petals and flowers, is a pot-pourri of colour and, when the lid is taken off, perfume too. The effect is informal, even amusing—why not?*

SIZE
74 cm × 51 cm (29 in × 20 in).

CONTAINER
A china bowl 20 cm (8 in) in diameter and 9 cm (3½ in) high.

EQUIPMENT
An oblong block of dry foam impaled on a small pinholder, standing 4 cm (1½ in) above the rim, taped to the bowl.

FOLIAGE
Bracken fern, purchased, dyed brown and shaded red, pressed.
Glycerined
 *Eucalyptus gunnii* (adult foliage) (cider gum).

FLOWERS
Air dried
 *Amaranthus hypochondriacus* (prince's feather).
 *Eryngium amethystinum* (sea holly).
 *Gypsophila paniculata* (baby's breath, chalk plant), dyed red.
 *Limonium sinuatum* (notch-leaf or winged statice).

GRASS
*Cortaderia conspicua* (pampas grass), air dried.

SEEDHEADS
*Lunaria annua (L. biennis)* (honesty, satin flower, moonwort), stripped of outer seedcases, air dried.

ACCESSORY
A glass jar 30½ cm × 14 cm (12 in × 5½ in), filled with a generous amount of dried flower heads and pot-pourri.

ARRANGER
Joan Dunne

*1* Fill the jar carefully with layer upon layer of stemless flowers, petals and perfumed pot-pourri, making sure that attractive and varied shapes and colours show through the glass all the way up. A jar of this size takes a lot of filling, so a round of dry foam can be put in and the first layers worked around it (make sure it is hidden).

*2* For the arrangement in the bowl, start with central stems of the paler pink statice and, in front, place a tall stem of the honesty. Then take short pieces of pampas, arranging these round the bowl, higher at the left and at the back than on the right and with pieces coming forwards over the rim. Next add the sprays of fern, using them behind the statice and honesty but shorter, add more lower on both sides. Place fern also out towards the back on the left, forward at the front and out on the right.

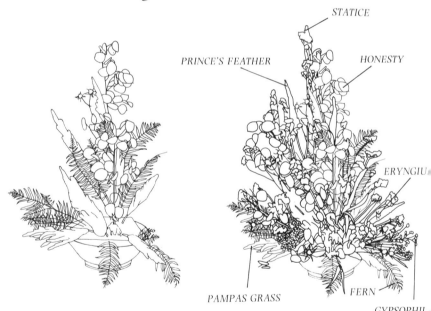

STATICE

PRINCE'S FEATHER

HONESTY

ERYNGIU

PAMPAS GRASS

FERN

GYPSOPHIL

*3* Add the darker statice and a few stems of spiky eryngium around the outline. Take a stem of honesty and two of amaranthus out to the left and place another, shorter, stem of honesty lower on the same side. Next fill in the centre starting with stems of amaranthus and honesty, shortening each as you work down towards the bowl. Following this line, add more of the paler statice and tuck in a few eryngium stems and the narrow eucalyptus leaves for contrast. Low on the left place sprays of the dark red gypsophila and, on the right, in front of the jar, add another stem of amaranthus, more gypsophila and, at the back, a little more eucalyptus.

# ARRANGEMENTS OF FRESH AND EVERLASTING FLOWERS

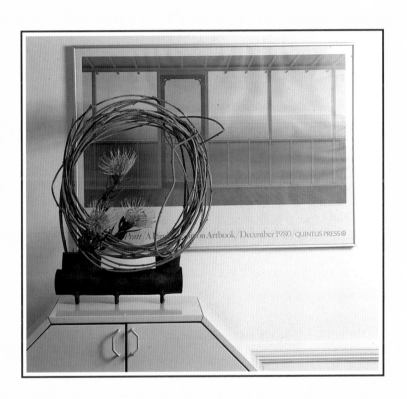

Pratt / A Fine Communication Artbook / December 1980 / QUINTUS PRESS ®

# ART NOUVEAU

*The apparent simplicity of this design is one of its charms. The twisting stems with their tiny seedheads and the decoration of the white woodwork suggest movement. The lilies and the pottery dish have shape in common but contrasting textures. The finished arrangement reminds us of the Art Nouveau period, the time when this home with its decorative fireplace was built.*

*SIZE*
76 cm × 38 cm (30 in × 15 in).

*CONTAINER*
Free-form pottery bowl, 15 cm (6 in) high × 25 cm (10 in) across the top.

*EQUIPMENT*
A pinholder, 10 cm (4 in) in diameter. A round of foam placed on the pinholder towards the front and the right.

*FOLIAGE*
From the flower stems.

*FLOWERS*
Fresh
  *Lilium longiflorum* (white trumpet or Easter lily).

*SEED-HEADS*
Air dried
  *Papaver* (poppy).

*ARRANGER*
Pamela South

*1* Carefully consider and then cut the poppy stems at various lengths. Place them on the pinholder, grouping them to make an interesting pattern against the white background. (Before placing the seedheads protect the cut stem ends with waterproof tape or varnish to the depth of the water in the bowl.)

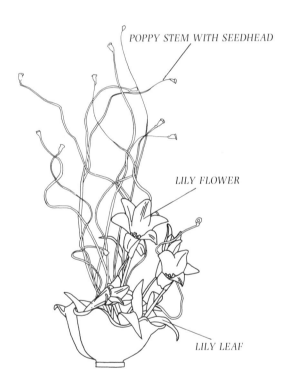

POPPY STEM WITH SEEDHEAD

LILY FLOWER

LILY LEAF

*2* Take a stem of lilies and use the shorter stems of the flowers and buds separately, putting these in the foam. Place a bud out towards the back at the right, a fully open flower above and nearer the centre, facing forwards, a half-open flower on the right again, this shorter and facing forwards, and then an opening bud near the rim of the bowl, this time coming from the pinholder and facing to the right. Leave a few of the dark, glossy green leaves on the stems and place two to curve out over the rim of the bowl.

# PICKED TO KEEP

*Hydrangeas, with their petal-like bracts, are one of the most successful
subjects for drying in shallow water and here they are used in a bold
arrangement which can be changed to suit them as they dry off, becoming
papery and attractively subtle in their more subdued colourings. The fresh
foliage can be replaced by preserved leaves and seedheads or by evergreens, so
varying the effect through the early winter.*

**1** The slender iris leaves will establish the height and width of the arrangement and these should be used first. The tallest leaf curves up from the centre of the foam to finish a little to the left of the centre. The width can be given with a leaf used low on either side, the left a little higher than the right. In between, place shorter stems of the weigela and a few more iris leaves. Follow on with seven modestly sized pale hydrangeas, confirming the flow of the design from the top down towards the hearth on the right. Balance the design with two more hydrangea heads by the iris leaf on the left and one coming well forward at the front.

*SIZE*
99 cm × 117 cm (39 in × 46 in).

*CONTAINER*
A brass coal-scuttle 25½ cm (10 in) high and 25½ cm (10 in) in diameter.

*EQUIPMENT*
A round baking tin, 18 cm (7 in) in diameter × 5 cm (2 in) deep. This stands on a log of wood which raises it to 5 cm (2 in) below the scuttle rim. A 10 cm (4 in) pinholder with a piece of foam trimmed to fit across the tin, leaving room to top up with water easily at the back or front. The foam stands 7½ cm (3 in) above the scuttle's rim.

*FOLIAGE*
Fresh
    *Fatsia japonica (Aralia sieboldii)* (Japanese fatsia, false castor oil plant).
    *Hosta sieboldiana* 'Frances Williams' ('Gold Edge').
    *Iris pseudacorus* 'Variegata'.
    *Weigela florida (Diervilla florida)* 'Variegata'.

*FLOWERS*
To dry
    *Hydrangea macrophylla (H. hortensia)* (mop-headed hydrangea).
Dried
    *Delphinium consolida* (larkspur) 'Giant Imperial' strain.

*SEEDHEADS*
To dry
    *Phlomis samia*
(Suitable replacements for the foliage and additional seedheads include: glycerine-preserved fatsia and aspidistra leaves; evergreens, such as conifers and *Phormium tenax*; dried pressed ferns, glycerined beech sprays and slender crocosmia leaves; dried crocosmia seedheads and various iris seed-pods.

*ARRANGER*
Margaret Newman

**2** Next take the bold fatsia and hosta leaves and use these nearer the middle, the fatsias on the left and the hostas brought through and following again the curving line down to the right. Against these hostas use three of the larger, darker hydrangeas and another, smaller one, low on the right. Remember to recess some and bring others forward a little. Add another pale hydrangea head up on the left and tuck a small one in at the middle between the two largest blooms.

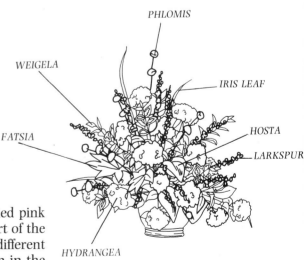

**3** To give lightness to the design, add the spikes of air-dried pink larkspur around the outline, some coming from the heart of the arrangement; vary the stem lengths. Finish with the very different form and colour of the drying phlomis seedheads, using them in the same way. Do not forget to protect the ends of the dried material before putting it into the wet foam.

# PROTEAS

*A circle of wisteria, pliable when fresh, makes a frame for the fresh proteas,
subtle in colour but bold in their form. These too will dry successfully. The
soft shades of the framed print are repeated by the flowers and stems, and the
horizontal and vertical lines appear again in the container. Without the
circling stem much of the impact of this design would be lost and the way in
which it is placed to the left of the picture is important.*

*SIZE*
61 cm × 46 cm (24 in × 18 in).

*CONTAINER*
Modern stoneware, $35\frac{1}{2}$ cm (14 in) long,
15 cm (6 in) high, with two openings,
10 cm (4 in) in diameter and $5\frac{1}{2}$ cm ($2\frac{1}{2}$ in) in
diameter.

*EQUIPMENT*
A small pinholder, $7\frac{1}{2}$ cm (3 in) in diameter.

*FLOWERS*
Fresh
  *Protea* (possibly *P. palongiflora* or a
  hybrid).

*OTHER PLANT MATERIAL*
Stem of *Wisteria sinensis* (*W. chinensis*)
(Chinese wisteria), coiled and then air dried.

*ARRANGER*
Pamela South

PROTEA

WISTERIA STEM

1 Fix the end of the coiled wisteria stem to the pinholder which is then placed in the larger of the two openings; the smaller opening supports the circle.

2 The stems of the three heavy-headed proteas are cut at different lengths and threaded through the wisteria and then pressed on to the pinholder. A short slit into each stem end makes this easier. The tallest flower, although angled towards the right, should face up and to the left. Place one lower, coming forward and very slightly right, and the third flower out to the right, to be seen almost in profile.

on Artbook/December 1980/QUINTUS PRESS ⊗

# THE MIDAS TOUCH

*Glowing colours of both fresh and preserved flowers with foliage and a few
berries, are mixed together generously in a large copper jug, standing on a
brass-tray-topped folding table. These late summer flowers have been
arranged against a framework of leaves which, as the flowers fade, will still
provide a background for fresh replacements or for other everlasting flowers,
foliage and seedheads.*

*1* Take the stems of glycerined beech first and form the outline: a
graceful tall piece for the centre top, two shorter pieces to flow
down at each side, and a fourth spray coming forward at the front.
Add the dark brown mahonia leaves towards the centre to show up
clearly against the paler beech (if the former are wiped over *very*
lightly with a little salad oil they will have a richer sheen). Next use
the three aspidistra leaves, to the left, to the right and down to the left
again; they will give a contrasting, simple shape. Add the sprays of
box (bleached by sunlight), with its small, densely placed, pale leaves
behind but close to the aspidistras.

*2* Next add the flat heads of the achillea towards the centre of the
design, recessing some, and follow with sprays of alchemilla. At
this stage very little more would be needed to complete an everlasting
arrangement. However, to suit the late summer mood, add a few
sprays of berries—the hypericum with its fresh green leaves will add a
lively note before the fresh flowers are added.

*3* Add gladioli for height and the dahlias in their various shapes
and shades towards the outside, with 'Preference' grouped on
the left. Above these dahlias add the roses, 'Typhoon' and 'Whisky
Mac', then place one more dahlia in the centre and another 'Whisky
Mac' to the right. Tuck sprays of the chrysanthemum in at the sides to
give depth to the design and interest when the arrangement is seen
from a different angle. Finish by adding the richly coloured lilies at
both sides of the top rose.

*SIZE*
97 cm × 86 cm (39 in × 34 in).

*CONTAINER*
An antique copper jug, 27 cm (10½ in) tall
and 19 cm (7½ in) in diameter at the foot and
16½ cm (6½ in) in diameter at the lip.

*EQUIPMENT*
Plastic dish with block of foam 12½ × 12½ ×
10 cm (5 × 5 × 4 in). Tape to secure.

*FOLIAGE*
Glycerined
   *Aspidistra elatior* (cast-iron plant).
   *Buxus sempervirens (common box).*
   *Fagus sylvatica* (common beech).
   *Mahonia bealei* (leatherleaf mahonia).

*FLOWERS*
Glycerined
   *Alchemilla mollis* (lady's mantle).
Air dried
   *Achillea filipendulina* 'Gold Plate' (fern-
   leaved yarrow).
Fresh
   Chrysanthemum (florists' spray variety).
   Dahlias 'Katisha', 'Andrea's Orange',
   'Paul Chester', 'Preference'. Gladiolus
   'Peter Pears'. Lily 'Festival'. Roses
   'Typhoon', 'Whisky Mac'.

*BERRIES*
*Hypericum androsaemum* (St John's wort,
tutsan), fresh.

*ARRANGER* Valerie Ford

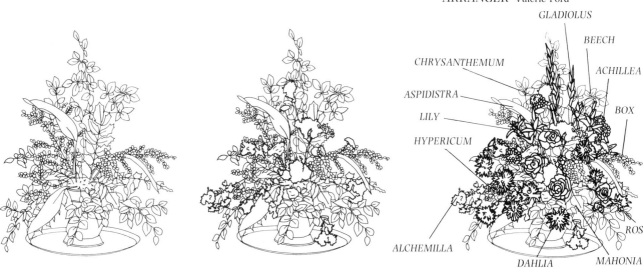

# SPRINGTIME AND DRIFTWOOD

*A favourite piece of weathered and dried wood has been used as the framework for an arrangement of leaves and just a few early spring flowers— an interesting combination of fresh and everlasting. All the flowers and most of the leaves are on quite short stems but by using the wood an arrangement has been created which is in scale with its setting.*

*SIZE*
150 cm (59 in) high and 117 cm (46 in) at floor level.

*CONTAINER*
A piece of dry, weathered wood, 80 cm (31 in) high.

*EQUIPMENT*
Two small round tins, 6 cm ($2\frac{1}{2}$ in) in diameter and 3 cm ($1\frac{1}{4}$ in) deep. Two squares of soaked foam standing 4 cm ($1\frac{1}{2}$ in) above the rims. A plastic plant saucer, 16 cm (6 in) in diameter. A square of well-soaked foam standing 5 cm (2 in) above the rim. A putty substance. Two glass bloom-holders (for hellebores).

*FLOWERS*
Fresh
   *Freesia refracta* 'Ballerina'.
   *Helleborus lividus corsicus (H. argutifolius)* (Corsican hellebore).
   *Helleborus orientalis* (Lenten hellebore, Lenten rose).
   *Hyacinthus romanus (Bellevalia romana)* (Roman hyacinth).

*FOLIAGE*
Fresh
   *Arum italicum* 'Pictum'.
   *Bergenia purpurascens (B. delavayi, B. beesiana) (Megasia)*.
   *Cleyera fortunei* 'Tricolor'.
   *Euphorbia amygdaloides* 'Purpurea' (purple wood spurge).
   *Heuchera americanum* 'Palace Purple' (alum root, rock geranium).
   *Iris pseudacorus* (yellow flag iris).
   *Nandina domestica* (heavenly bamboo).
   *Sarcococca hookeriana humilis* (sweet box).
   *Tellima grandiflora (T. odorata)* (fringecup).
Ferns
   *Adiantum venustum (A. microphyllum)* (maidenhair fern).
   *Phyllitis scolopendrium (Scolopendrium vulgare)* 'Crispum' (hart's-tongue fern).
   *Polystichum setiferum* (soft shield or hedge fern).
   *Polystichum setiferum* 'Plumoso-divisilobum'.

*ARRANGER*
Joan Dunne

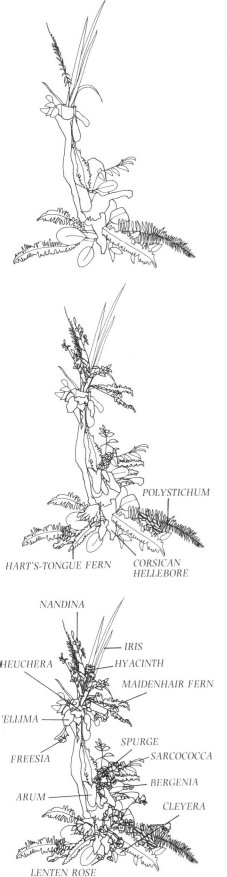

HART'S-TONGUE FERN     CORSICAN
                          HELLEBORE

POLYSTICHUM

NANDINA

HEUCHERA

IRIS

HYACINTH

MAIDENHAIR FERN

TELLIMA

SPURGE

SARCOCOCCA

FREESIA

BERGENIA

ARUM

CLEYERA

LENTEN ROSE

*1* Stand the wood at an angle and then place the plant saucer on the floor behind the front leg of the wood. Attach the two small tins with the putty and then with tape. Make sure they are secure and horizontal, the first behind the right-hand branch and the second just behind the topmost point. These tins will be small enough to hide with the leaves but they will need to be regularly recharged with water. With three iris leaves establish the height from the top tin. To their left, place a frond of *Polystichum setiferum* fern. From the plant saucer create balancing width with both kinds of the polystichum ferns and, on the right, add a spray of the cream-edged cleyera. In the middle section place a piece of the polystichum fern to the right of the wood. Next add the oval bergenia leaves, three in the lowest group, one from the right just below the short branch, another forward at floor level and slightly to the left and the third of these leaves out to the left. Above, in the next group, add two more smaller leaves, one following the line of the short branch and one behind to the right of the fern. At the top, add short sprays of the cleyera on the left and lower on the right.

*2* Build up the three groups of foliage, starting with larger and bolder leaves at the base and smaller and daintier in the other two sections. Use the nandina on the left at the top and on the right but slightly back in the middle section. Suggest a line through the whole design with the cream-veined arums, grading them in size, bringing one well down over the wood in the middle. Add bold stems of the purplish spurge at both sides of the bottom group and a shorter piece in the centre of the middle group. In a similar way add the crinkled-edge leaves of the hart's-tongue fern. In the top section use tellima and heuchera leaves, bringing them forward and down to hide the tin. Above the arum and out to the back, add the dark green, small-leaved sarcococca. Use more in the heart of the middle section. With the maidenhead fern introduce a feathery texture. At the top place it in front of the iris leaves; in the middle, out to the right by the branch; at the base, out to the left from the angle in the wood.

*3* Now add a few flowers. First use the white freesias, making use of their curving stems: three at the top; three curving through the centre section; two out to the right, coming from behind the wood, in the lowest section; then one in the centre and one in front of the maidenhair fern. Add more white with the stems of Roman hyacinths, starting at the top with one in front of the iris and another curving to the right. In the next group, place just one near the centre. From the plant saucer use a hyacinth to link this with the group above by placing it in front of the wood and near to the right-hand arum leaf. Place the last of these flowers low down and towards the right. Add a cluster of green hellebore flowers (in a water-filled bloom-holder) between the last two hyacinths and then the pinkish-green hellebores (in their bloom-holder) at the very front. Their colour will pick up the darker colour of the wood spurge. In the finished arrangement the wood remains an important part of the whole design.

# A GIFT OF
# FLOWERS

*A charming gift of mixed fresh and everlasting flowers arranged in a little
china candlestick, the colours chosen as carefully as the lacy textured
flowers. The roses, leaves and grasses pick up the details of the setting on the
bedside table.*

64

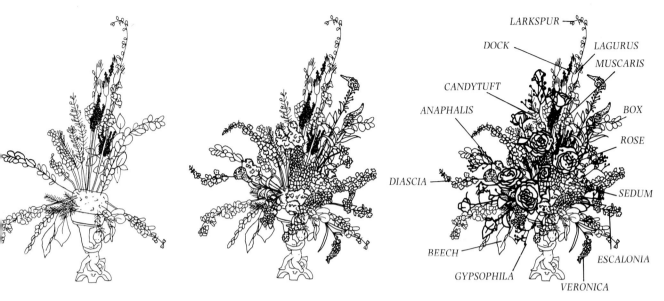

LARKSPUR
DOCK
LAGURUS
MUSCARIS
CANDYTUFT
ANAPHALIS
BOX
ROSE
DIASCIA
SEDUM
BEECH
ESCALONIA
GYPSOPHILA
VERONICA

*SIZE*
55 cm × 37 cm (22 in × 15 in).

*CONTAINER*
A white china cupid candlestick, 12½ cm
(5 in) high.

*EQUIPMENT*
A white plastic candle-cup holder with a
block of foam. This is fixed in the candlestick
at a slight angle with a putty substance and
taped to secure the foam to the candle-cup.

*FOLIAGE*
Glycerined
  *Fagus sylvatica* (common beech).
  *Buxus sempervirens* (common box).
  *Taxus baccata* (common or English yew).

*FLOWERS*
Air dried
  *Anaphalis triplinervis* (pearly everlasting).
  *Delphinium consolida* (common larkspur,
  annual delphinium).
  *Rumex obtusifolius* (broad-leaved dock).
  *Lagurus ovatus* (hare's-tail grass, rabbit's-
  tail grass).
Fresh
  *Diascia cordata*.
  *Escallonia × rigida* 'Donard Seedling'.
  *Gypsophila paniculata* 'Rosy Veil' (baby's
  breath, chalk plant).
  *Polygonum affine* (knotweed, fleece flower).
  Roses 'Garnette' and 'Garnette Carol'.
  *Sedum spectabile* 'Ruby Glow' (ice plant).
  *Veronica spicata* 'Snow White' (spiked
  speedwell).

*SEEDHEADS*
Air dried
  *Iberis sempervirens* (perennial candytuft).
  *Muscaris botryoides* (common grape
  hyacinth).

*1* Place a tall, slender stem of larkspur buds out a little to the right at the top and two more low down, one on either side. These three stems will be a guide to the shape of the finished arrangement. Follow, now, with the grasses, grouped together near the top. In the centre line, near the top, place a muscaris seedhead. Add candytuft seedheads, just below on the left, and some more leaning over the rim of the container. Then put in two pieces of box on the right and tuck two more in on the left. Place short sprays of beech leaves out towards the back behind the box on the right, near the lamp and low on the left. Next add the dark dock spikes by the grasses and a few pieces of both the dark and the pale pink larkspur. A little of the dark brown glycerined yew, tucked in near the centre, repeats the brown of the dock; use some more to cover the foam at the back. Another interesting touch can be added with pieces of the dark purple-brown sedum used at the sides towards the back.

*2* Apart from the sedum the basis of the arrangement is of everlastings. Add the white anaphalis high and low in the middle and another stem out to the left. Now add the fresh flowers. Use the spikes of white veronica and pink diascia round the sides. Build up both the centre and the outline with sprigs of escallonia and add a few polygonum flowers to give more depth of pink in the centre of the arrangement. Tuck in a muscaris seedhead between the escallonia sprigs on the right.

*3* Complete the arrangement with the roses and the gysophila. Place the darker and more open roses towards the middle and the buds, in profile, nearer the outside. The fluffy sprays of pink gypsophila should be used to give a lacy finish to this special gift.

*ARRANGER*
Valerie Ford

# ARRANGEMENTS FOR THANKSGIVING AND THE CHRISTMAS SEASON

# THANKSGIVING
# GARLAND

*The garland of fruits, nuts, cones, flowers and leaves is specially created for Thanksgiving Day. The circle can be hung, as you see it here, on a wall or door, or it can be used as a table centre.*

*SIZE*
The circle is 48 cm (19 in) in diameter.

*EQUIPMENT*
A circular wreath frame, 40½ cm (16 in) in diameter, with dry foam. Glue. Fine wires and fine bamboo skewers. Florist's tape. Red ribbon, 2½ cm (1 in) wide. Red ribbon (which tears lengthways) for bows. Spray paints, gold, matt white and other colours.

*FOLIAGE*
Glycerined
   *Alchemilla mollis* (lady's mantle).
   *Eucalyptus gunnii* (gum tree).
   *Fagus sylvatica* (common beech).
   *Grevillea robusta* (silky oak).
   *Mahonia aquifolium* (Oregon grape).
   *Quercus robur* (English oak).
   *Skimmia japonica.*
   *Humulus lupulus* (hop), picked and treated while green but mature.

*FLOWERS AND GRASSES*
Air dried
   *Achillea filipendulina* (fern-leaved yarrow).
   *Alchemilla mollis* (lady's mantle).
   *Helichrysum bracteatum* (strawflower, everlasting daisy).
   Wheat ears.

*FRUITS, NUTS, AND GALLS*
Dried in netting bag in airing cupboard
   Gourds, lemons, pomegranates, tangerines, chestnuts, peach stones, pecans, walnuts, oak apples.

*CONES*
*Alnus glutinosa* (black or common European alder).
*Cedrus atlantica* (Atlas cedar).
*Larix decidua* (European larch).

*ARRANGER*
Brenda Evans

*PREPARATION*
**1** Drill the fruit and the nuts with a fine drill; it will be possible, then, to fix them in the arrangement with a fine bamboo skewer.

Give the large dried fruits a spray with matt white paint before spraying with appropriate colours—more than one to give shaded effects. The white paint undercoat helps to give a brighter finish. The gourds come in many shapes and can be chosen to look like different fruits—pears, peaches and so on.

Wire the alder cones into bunches and spray them lightly with gold (see page 122).

Spray the wheat ears and oak apples with gold and lightly tip-spray the mahonia.

Cut the cedar cones across to make 'roses' and give them wire stems. Wire the larch cones.

Wire loops of ribbon and make into bows.

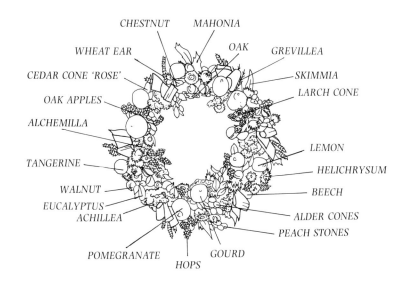

CHESTNUT   MAHONIA
WHEAT EAR   OAK   GREVILLEA
CEDAR CONE 'ROSE'   SKIMMIA
OAK APPLES   LARCH CONE
ALCHEMILLA
LEMON
TANGERINE   HELICHRYSUM
WALNUT   BEECH
EUCALYPTUS   ALDER CONES
ACHILLEA   PEACH STONES
POMEGRANATE   GOURD
HOPS

2 Take the wreath frame and glue a length of $2\frac{1}{2}$ cm (1 in) wide ribbon round the edge. Then cover the foam with individually placed beech leaves, each one held in place with a hairpin-like wire. This gives a good base for the colourful material. Next add wired sprays of hops at random around the circle. Take some of the large fruit and use it in three equidistant groupings. Add to the design by filling in with bright yellow achillea, alchemilla, helichrysum, smaller fruits and foliage. Use the wheat and mahonia around the outside. Six red bows will complete the circle.

# THANKSGIVING DAY DINNER

*Here is an idea for a table decoration which can be adapted for other celebrations, but it is designed here for a Thanksgiving party using flowers, fruits and baubles in the coppery colours which seem so right in November. The slender candles give height without detracting from the small flowers.*

## SIZE
63½ cm (25 in) in diameter.

## EQUIPMENT
Two round cake boards, 45½ cm (18 in) and 30½ cm (12 in) in diameter, covered smoothly in silver fabric. Three plant-pot saucers, one 15 cm (6 in) and two 10 cm (4 in) in diameter. A small round of wet foam, 7½ cm (3 in) in diameter and 5 cm (2 in) high. Two lengths of wet foam, crumbled and then packed to shape, wrapped in kitchen foil, reverse (dull) side out, one 183 cm (72 in) long, the other 96 cm (38 in) long, both 4 cm (1½ in) in diameter.

## FOLIAGE
Glycerined
  *Buxus sempervirens* (box).
  *Camellia reticulata.*
  *Fagus sylvatica* (European beech).
  *Quercus rubra* (red oak).
  Ferns, purchased.

## FLOWERS
Fresh
  Roses, spray carnations and spray chrysanthemums, florists' varieties in shades of apricot, pale pink and copper.
Air dried
  *Gypsophila elegans* (baby's breath), white, sprayed silver.
  *Protea*, small type purchased as 'bridal' proteas.
  Made-up (contrived) flowers of honesty seedpots and small cones (see page 123).

## SEEDHEADS
*Eucalyptus globulus* (Tasmanian blue gum), purchased, sprayed silver.

## ACCESSORIES
Five slender flower candles, apricot-coloured, mounted on cocktail sticks, two to each candle and attached with sticky tape. Copper baubles, wired individually. A bunch of artificial grapes, bronze-coloured, separated and wired singly. Tiny cherub figures, sprayed bronze. Table mats covered to match base boards. Silver and apricot-coloured crackers. Apricot-coloured napkins.

## ARRANGER
Jill Findlay

**1** In the middle of the table place the larger board on top of the largest plant saucer (upturned). Use one of the smaller saucers in the same way to raise the second board and on this, still centrally, place the third saucer holding the round of wet foam. Lay the lengths of foam-filled foil round both boards, just tucked under securely. Add the candles in the top section.

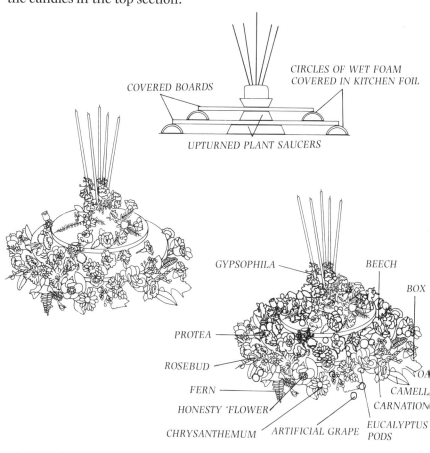

CIRCLES OF WET FOAM COVERED IN KITCHEN FOIL
COVERED BOARDS
UPTURNED PLANT SAUCERS

GYPSOPHILA
BEECH
BOX
PROTEA
ROSEBUD
OA
FERN
CAMELL
HONESTY 'FLOWER'
CARNATION
CHRYSANTHEMUM
ARTIFICIAL GRAPE
EUCALYPTUS PODS

**2** Work round both circles and on the top part of the design with the foliage, the bolder leaves being placed nearest to the table and the daintier further up, with the box and the ferns at the top. Add the flowers, all on quite short stems, the larger and darker at the bottom, going up to the palest and the buds. Use the sprays of gypsophila at all levels, finishing with a little, kept low, among the candles. The flowers made from the honesty pods should be worked into the design on the lowest and the middle levels.

**3** Among the flowers add the silvered eucalyptus fruits, the copper baubles and the individually wired grapes. Place the little cherubs around the two silver boards.

# ADVENT

*A delicate arrangement, perfectly suiting the little table. The colour scheme is unusual, with the clear yellow of the berries, the touches of gold repeating the shining candlestick and the importance of the dark green candle among the greens and browns of the leaves and seedheads.*

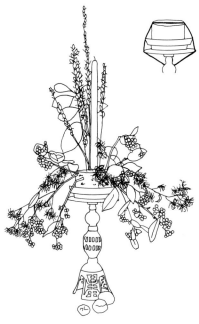

*1* The foxglove seedheads and the candle should be placed first, the slender seedheads towards the back and the candle about two-thirds back. Mount the candle on the cocktail sticks with the adhesive tape so that it will not split the foam or take up too much room. Add a spray of the brown, glycerined camellia foliage behind the seedheads. At the front, bring shorter pieces of the camellia forward and down to mask the foam and to provide a dark but interesting background. Using both the pyracantha berries and the glycerined wild clematis, add delicate shapes and patterns low on both sides of the arrangement and then two shorter stems of berries a little higher.

## SIZE
79 cm × 48 cm (31 in × 19 in).

## CONTAINER
A decorative brass candlestick, 27 cm (10½ in) tall with a plastic dish attached, 12 cm (4¾ in) in diameter.

## EQUIPMENT
A round of well-soaked foam, taped securely to the plastic dish and then to the candlestick.

## FOLIAGE
Fresh
   *Camellia japonica.*
   *Hedera helix* (ivy).

## FLOWERS
*Alchemilla mollis* (lady's mantle), air dried.

## SEEDHEADS
Glycerined
   *Clematis vitalba* (wild clematis, old man's beard).
   *Digitalis lutea* (perennial foxglove).
Air dried
   *Clematis vitalba* (wild clematis, traveller's joy, old man's beard).
   Iris.

## BERRIES
*Pyracantha atalantioides* 'Aurea', fresh.
Rosehips, painted gold, glycerined.

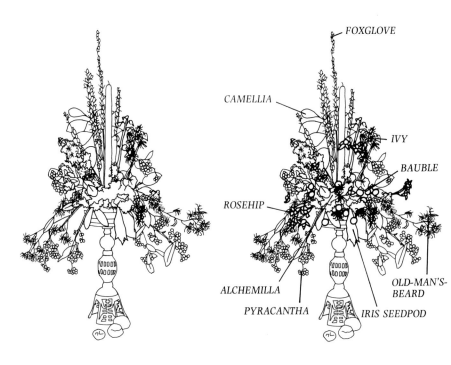

*2* To give a little boldness in the heart of the design, add a few of the ivy leaves—the rich dark green will show through well. Low on the left place a short piece of camellia. Add the yellow alchemilla above this, as well as through the centre and out to the right. On both sides use a little more clematis, with a fluffy dried piece on the left.

72

*ACCESSORIES*
A green candle, 30 cm (12 in) tall. Four
cocktail sticks (or matches) and transparent
adhesive tape. Golden baubles, the larger
ones given wire stems.

*ARRANGER*
Mary Graves

*3* Complete the arrangement with the gilded rosehips in a well
spaced group on the left and another stem out to the right. Give
a tiny gold bauble to the tip of each hip. Fill in the middle with the
larger golden baubles and a few feathery pieces of the clematis set
among the shorter pieces of alchemilla. Take great care not to
overcrowd this design.

# EVERGREEN

*The swag and tree here combine to welcome visitors with a Christmas message of good wishes. Over the door is the evergreen swag with just a little dried material added. The traditional holly has been used with golden wheat to suggest prosperity, yew for a long life, bunches of alder fruit to suggest grapes for an abundant harvest and flowers made to resemble Christmas roses (Helleborus niger). The door hanging, in the form of a little Christmas tree, continues the message offering a happy welcome to a country home.*

## THE SWAG

### SIZE
Made in four parts: above the door, each 46 cm (18 in) long and wired to the drops, 26½ cm (10½ in) long, excluding the ribbons.

### EQUIPMENT
Chicken wire, 2½ cm (1 in) mesh, cut to a width of 18 cm (7 in) and of measured lengths for each section required; this is shaped into tubes, filled with damp moss and secured firmly with the ends sealed. Curtain rings for joining the sections and for hanging (wired to the back of the chicken-wire forms, two at the top of each horizontal piece and one at the top of each drop), these are attached before the plant material is added. Florist's wires; latex adhesive; a polythene strip taped in place, at the back, over the chicken wire to neaten; gold spray paint. Approximately 1 metre (40 in) of 2½ cm (1 in) wide red velvet ribbon.

### FOLIAGE
Fresh
Araucaria araucana (monkey puzzle).
Cupressus (cypress).
Ilex aquifolium 'Argenteo-marginata' (variegated holly).
Taxus baccata (yew).
Palm leaflets (pressed).

### CONES
Abies alba (European silver fir).
Alnus glutinosa (alder).

### SEEDHEADS
Air dried
Eryngium giganteum.
Fagus sylvatica (common beech), cupules.
Lunaria annua (honesty).
Papaver somniferum (poppy).
Wheat ears.

### ARRANGER Wendy Bailey

1 Prepare everything before assembling the various parts of the decoration and allocate the stock to ensure an even balance when the design is complete. Give short stems of florist's wire to the poppy heads, the wheat, the cones, the beech cupules and 'stars' made from cuts across the monkey puzzle foliage. Doing this will make it much easier to get each piece firmly in place in the moss. Form single loops from the palm fronds and give these short wire stems. Spray the eryngium heads and all the wired material with gold paint. Spray the yew very lightly. Make flowers from the honesty seed cases by gluing them, as petals, into the smaller fir cones which have already been wired; very carefully spray just the edges of these petals. Cluster the gilded and wired alder fruits into little bunches to resemble grapes.

2 Cover the edges of the moss-filled wire frames with pieces of cupressus; lay these along the forms, overlapping, towards the outer ends and carefully wire them in place. Build up the design with the other foliage, adding the gilded material and the flowers last. Make sure there is more width in the centres of the horizontal pieces than at the ends and taper the shape carefully for the drops—finish these with the gilded wheat ears and the streamers of ribbon.

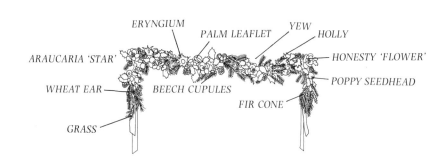

ERYNGIUM — PALM LEAFLET — YEW — HOLLY — ARAUCARIA 'STAR' — HONESTY 'FLOWER' — WHEAT EAR — BEECH CUPULES — POPPY SEEDHEAD — FIR CONE — GRASS

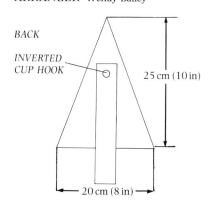

BACK
INVERTED CUP HOOK
25 cm (10 in)
20 cm (8 in)

1 Assemble all the material, wiring and spraying as for the swag before starting. Construct the tree-shaped background and add the foam and wire. Work with the cupressus and spruce first, covering all the equipment but carefully keeping the tree shape. If this base is kept damp it can· be made some time before it is needed and the decorations added at the last minute—just a few baubles and ribbons and, in this case, three honesty 'flowers' and a red ribbon.

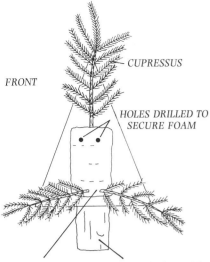

FRONT

CUPRESSUS

HOLES DRILLED TO
SECURE FOAM

FOAM, WRAPPED
IN POLYTHENE
AND COVERED IN
CHICKEN WIRE

LARCH BRANCH HELD
IN POSITION WITH
SCREWS OR STRONG
GLUE

## THE TREE

### SIZE
43 cm (17 in) high and 28 cm (11 in) at the
widest point.

### EQUIPMENT
A triangle of hardboard, 25 cm × 20 cm
(10 in × 8 in). Thin wood to stiffen, 33 cm ×
5 cm (13 in × 2 in). A small cup hook. A
halved branch of *Larix decidua (L. europaea)*
(European larch), approximately 12 cm
(5 in) long and 5 cm (2 in) across. A block of
wet foam wrapped in thin polythene,
$12\frac{1}{2}$ cm × 5 cm × $2\frac{1}{2}$ cm (5 in × 2 in × 1 in).
Chicken wire, $1\frac{1}{4}$ cm ($\frac{1}{2}$ in) mesh, to cover the
foam block; this is then wired to the centre
of the triangle.

## FOLIAGE
Fresh
   *Cupressus* (cypress).
   *Ilex aquifolium* 'Argenteo-marginata'
   (variegated holly).
   *Picea abies (P. excelsa)* (common or
   Norway spruce).

## CONES
*Larix decidua* (European larch).

## SEEDHEADS
Air dried
   *Papaver somniferum* (opium poppy).

## ARRANGER
Vivien Bolton

# THE CHRISTMAS STORY

*A richly colourful arrangement for Christmas. It is a mixture of fresh and dried plant material with some artificial flowers and leaves. The shining bergenia leaves and the pears make a central group against which the dried cones and helichrysums show up beautifully, and the colours of this treasured painting with its muted red and gold frame are repeated.*

*SIZE*
119½ cm wide × 109 cm (47 in × 43 in), including the ribbon.

*CONTAINER*
A round pottery bowl, 18 cm (7 in) in diameter and 9 cm (3½ in) deep.

*EQUIPMENT*
A heavy pinholder with a block of wet foam cut to stand 6½ cm (2½ in) above the rim. Wooden skewers or cocktail sticks. Florist's wires. Two red candles and low holders. Red velvet ribbon, 150 cm (5 ft) long and 4 cm (1½ in) wide.

*FOLIAGE*
Fresh
   *Bergenia (Megasia)* 'Ballawley' hybrid.
   *Ilex aquifolium* 'Golden King' (holly).
   *Tsuga heterophylla* (western hemlock).

*FLOWERS*
Air dried
   *Helichrysum bracteatum* (strawflower, everlasting daisy), sprayed lime-green, wired.

*OTHER PLANT MATERIAL*
Pine cones, wired.
Pears (fresh or artificial).

*ACCESSORIES*
Sprays of gold ivy leaves, purchased.
Sprays of gold flowers, purchased.
Red 'poinsettia' flowers on long wire stems, purchased.

*ARRANGER*
Joan Dunne

*1* Create the long flowing outline with the graceful hemlock, bringing it out to the sides, some slightly forward over the edge of the mantleshelf. To this add the two handsome bergenia leaves in the middle. Then add the bright green and yellow holly; with this follow the lines of the hemlock but cut the stems a little shorter.

*2* Add the gold and red next. Place sprays of the gold flowers low on either side, at the left a little longer than on the right, and add a third spray on the right, higher and out towards the wall. Emphasize the two lower sprays with the gold leaves and, to balance the design, use a third stem of the leaves up on the left. With the red flowers on their long stems, highlight the design but do not bring them right into the middle.

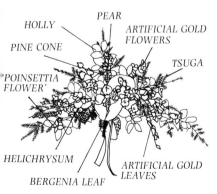

HOLLY
PINE CONE
'POINSETTIA FLOWER'
HELICHRYSUM
BERGENIA LEAF
PEAR
ARTIFICIAL GOLD FLOWERS
TSUGA
ARTIFICIAL GOLD LEAVES

*3* Put the pears on strong wooden skewers or use several cocktail sticks for each pear and anchor them in the foam as a central group. Next add the cones on strong wire stems, two forwards on the right of the pears, another above and a fourth low on the left. Above this last cone add a group of three or four lime-green helichrysum flowers; add another cluster above the top cone, a few more further out on the right and a final group between the front cones and the pears. Place the candles in their low holders on either side of the arrangement and cut the ribbon to make a loop and two tails. Give these wire stems and group them as a bow under the front glossy bergenia leaf. If a fire is to be lit, do not add the bow.

# POOLSIDE FANTASY

*An amusing setting for a Christmas arrangement. The green glass carboy is a
container in the same mood and this continues with the fantasy flowers and
the chime of glass bells linking the two parts of the design together.*

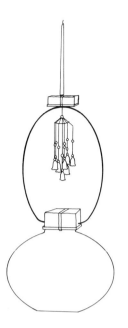

**1** First tie the cluster of bells in place at the top of the wire hoop, varying the lengths of the thread. Then attach the tins to their platforms. Place the candle in the centre of the foam at the top.

**2** Establish flowing, downward lines in both parts of the design. For the lower section pick curving stems of holly, both kinds of ivy and the chlorophytum. For the top, use the Boston fern around the candle to give the same shape but on a slightly smaller scale. Now, in both sections, fill in with shorter stems of holly, the ivies and the tree heath. Remember to work round at the back as well as the front of this arrangement as it will be seen from all sides, but do not let it become heavy and over-crowded. The grouped stems of variegated holly are especially important at the top. A spray of ivy should be taken up by the candle.

## SIZE
117 cm (46 in) high, including the candle, 99 cm (39 in) across, the top part 69 cm (27 in) across.

## CONTAINER
A carboy 33 cm (13 in) high and 41 cm (16 in) across, the type used for bottle gardens.

## EQUIPMENT
An oval of wire, covered with white tape, 46 cm (18 in) high with two metal platforms, one attached on the top and one inside at the bottom, the top 9 cm × 7½ cm (3½ in × 3 in), the bottom 11½ cm × 10 cm (4½ in × 4 in). Two oblong tins to fit platforms, and well soaked foam blocks standing 4 cm (1½ in) above their rims.

## FOLIAGE
Fresh
  *Asparagus plumosus* (asparagus fern).
  *Chlorophytum comosum* 'Vittatum' (spider plant, St Bernard's lily).
  *Erica arborea* 'Alpina' (tree heath).
  *Hedera helix* 'Glacier' (ivy).
  *Hedera canariensis* 'Gloire de Marengo' (Canary Island ivy).
  *Ilex aquifolium* 'Argenteo-marginata' (holly).
  *Nephrolepis exaltata* 'Bostoniensis' (Boston fern).
  *Polystichum aculeatum* (prickly or hard shield fern).

## ACCESSORIES
A green candle, mounted on four cocktail sticks with adhesive tape.
A cluster of glass bells.
Small, pale green baubles on individual wire stems. Larger, white, 'rayed' baubles on individual wire stems.

## ARRANGER
Pamela McNicol

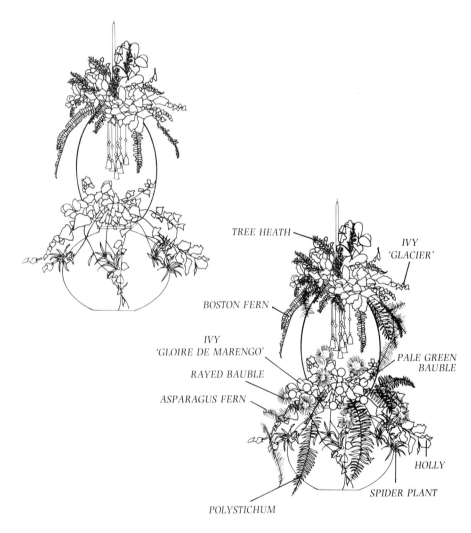

TREE HEATH
IVY 'GLACIER'
BOSTON FERN
IVY 'GLOIRE DE MARENGO'
RAYED BAUBLE
PALE GREEN BAUBLE
ASPARAGUS FERN
HOLLY
SPIDER PLANT
POLYSTICHUM

**3** In the lower section add a few trailing, feathery pieces of the asparagus fern and polystichum. Both should fall across and round the carboy. At the top, bring them down in a curve following the lines of the wire frame. Finish by adding the baubles, all in the lower section, the small green ones near the heart of the arrangement and the silver and white baubles, spaced out on their longer stems, to suggest fantasy Christmas flowers.

79

# CRIMSON AND GOLD

*At either end of this dark oak dresser the swags pick up the many different shades of red which decorate the farmhouse dining room. The gold adds a specially festive gleam but a little of the brown has been left to show through, giving a softer look. The design is made and assembled in three parts.*

## SIZE
Longer drop 91 cm (36 in); shorter drop 30½ cm (12 in); linking swag 61 cm (24 in).

## EQUIPMENT
Three lengths of strong wire (coat-hanger wire is suitable), 79 cm (31 in), 23 cm (9 in) and 66 cm (26 in). Two brass curtain rings for hanging the drops—the top swag is made to hook into the two rings when they are placed 61 cm (24 in) apart. Paint: gold spray; matt red; enamel red; enamel orange. Florist's tape (brown); silver reel wire; glue for attaching decorations; wire cutters and small scissors.

## FOLIAGE
Glycerined
  *Choisya ternata* (Mexican orange).
  *Fagus sylvatica* (common beech), gilded.
  *Olearia macrodonta* (daisy bush).
  *Ruscus aculeatus* (butcher's broom), sun bleached after glycerining.
  *Ruscus hypoglossum*, painted matt red.
  'Kaola', a florist's foliage from Australia, lightly gilded.

## FLOWERS
Air dried
  *Alchemilla mollis* (lady's mantle).

## CONES
*Abies alba* (European silver fir), lightly gilded at the edges.
*Alnus glutinosa* (alder).
*Larix decidua (L. europaea)* (European larch), gilded.
*Pinus sylvestris* (Scots pine), lightly gilded.

## SEEDHEADS
Air dried
  *Quercus robur* (English oak), acorns, some enamel-painted red.
  *Papaver somniferum* (opium poppy), some with their tops removed and enamel-painted red and orange and then sprayed gold. Some, with their tops left on, just sprayed gold.
  Wheat ears, gilded.

## OTHER PLANT MATERIAL
Toadstools, air dried in a warm atmosphere.
'Wood Rose', purchased.

## ARRANGER
Freda Williams

**1** Cover all three wires with the florist's tape, twisting between fingers and thumb. Make a hook at each end of the middle wire and curve it slightly until, from hook to hook, it is 61 cm (24 in) long. Make hooks at the top of the two drops and wire to the curtain rings. Except for those leaves which will be used to make the various types of flowers, all the material should be wired and the wires covered with tape.

**2** Make up two sets of the multi-coloured poppy heads as shown in diagram (a). These will be used to form the ends of the two drops. Next make a supply of the 'flowers', as in diagrams (b), (c) and (d). For (b) you will need about ten ruscus leaves which have been painted matt red. Glue these into the scales of a larch cone which has been painted red and gold. For smaller flowers and the suggestion of buds, put the leaves in on one side, or even less, of the cone. For flower (c), use the smaller variety of ruscus which has been bleached and glue into the alder cones in the same way. For flower (d), use the 'Kaola' leaves and glue these under the tops of the gilded poppy seedheads.

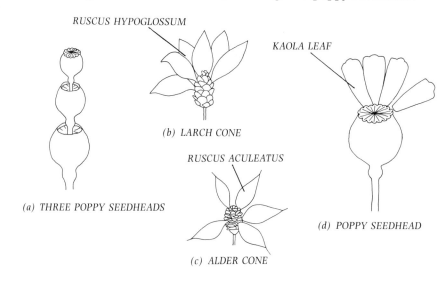

RUSCUS HYPOGLOSSUM

KAOLA LEAF

*(b) LARCH CONE*

RUSCUS ACULEATUS

*(a) THREE POPPY SEEDHEADS*

*(d) POPPY SEEDHEAD*

*(c) ALDER CONE*

**3** Assemble all three parts by carefully grading the sizes as you work. First glue the assembled poppy heads to the lowest ends of the drops. Gradually build up towards the top by taping on leaves, flowers and seedheads, keeping the largest and heaviest nearer to the centre line. Bend over the wire stalks on the last few leaves and these will hide the hooks at the top.

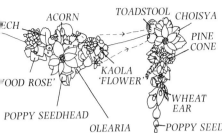

ECH    ACORN      TOADSTOOL   CHOISYA

                                 PINE
                                 CONE

'OOD ROSE'       KAOLA
               'FLOWER'

POPPY SEEDHEAD            WHEAT
                                EAR

       OLEARIA       POPPY SEEDHEAD DROP

For the central loop the work is started in the middle. Take care to work back from the centre towards both ends with similar material on both sides, gradually tapering to a neat finish, and again hiding the hooks. The leaves and seedheads should face slightly towards the centre as you tape them in place.

81

# RING OF WELCOME

*The unusual colours in this garland are enhanced by the sheen of the generously large moiré silk ribbon bow. It would look equally attractive hung against a dark background, maybe an oak front door.*

## SIZE
50½ cm (20 in) in diameter and 95 cm (37½ in) from the top leaf to the end of the longer streamer.

## EQUIPMENT
A hardboard circle, 48 cm (18 in) in diameter and inside measurement 30½ cm (12 in). Strong adhesive (the type used for bonding floor tiles) for attaching the heavier components, and a lighter gum for the others. Two metres (2¼ yards) gold-trimmed moiré ribbon.

## FOLIAGE
Glycerined
Camellia japonica.
Grevillea robusta (silky oak), gilded.
Magnolia grandiflora (bull bay, southern magnolia), bleached to a pale cream, purchased.
Pittosporum tenuifolium (P. mayi), gilded.
Rhododendron bureavii.
Ruscus aculeatus (butcher's broom), dyed lime green, purchased.

## FLOWERS
Made-up (contrived) flowers (see pages 122–123)—'Carnations' (corn-cob husks).
Carved balsa-wood flower.
Fantasy flowers (honesty seed-pods).
'Roses' (glycerined eucalyptus and ruscus foliage).

## BERRIES
Air dried
Physalis alkekengi (bladder cherry, Chinese lantern).
Sambucus nigra (elder).

## CONES
Cedrus libani (cedar of Lebanon), gilded.
Pinus silvestris (Scots pine), lightly gilded.

## GRASSES
Various species, air dried, including
Briza maxima (greater quaking grass), gilded.
Lagurus ovatus (hare's-tail grass, rabbit's-tail grass), some dyed.

## SEEDHEADS
Various air dried, including
Dipsacus fullonum (teasel), bleached then coloured mauve with spray paint.
Illicium verum (Chinese star anise).
Liquidambar styraciflua (sweet gum).

## NUTS
Carya illinoensis (pecan).

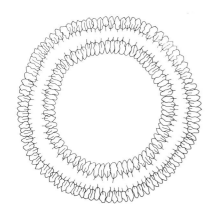

1 Lay the circle of hardboard on a flat working surface and have all the various components grouped and ready to use. Glue the pittosporum leaves in place first. Make sure both the inner and outer edges of the circle are adequately covered.

2 Work, next, on the top group in the design. Glue the larger leaves in place, magnolia at the back with camellia and rhododendron. Add the lime-green ruscus and gilded silky oak next, then the heavier material, a cone, teasel, corn and other seedheads. Below these, add two of the 'roses' and the carved wooden flower between them. Make sure these last three come down a little over the inner edge of the circle. Build up another group at the bottom of the circle, starting with the cream and lime green leaves. Fix the bow firmly behind the lowest leaves. In front of the leaves glue two corn-husk 'carnations' with a 'rose' between, lower and coming down into the centre of the bow. Next glue in place six of the aquamarine fantasy flowers, placed evenly, three on each side of the circle. Add lime-green ruscus at intervals around both the inner and outer edges of the circle.

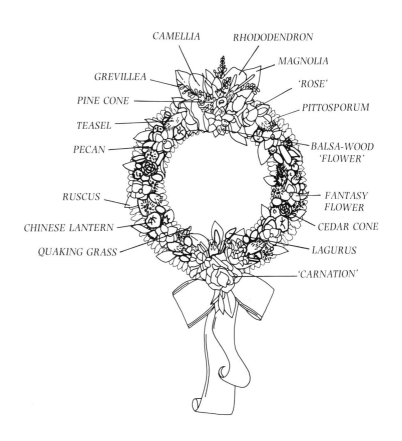

3 The garland is completed by filling in with the remaining material, but a regular pattern should be followed. Use the smaller material near the edges and the heavier and bolder material in the middle; this will help to give a neat and slightly domed finish. The pittosporum leaves should still show as a rich chestnut golden edging.

*ARRANGER*
Moira Macfarlane

# FOR FRIENDS AT CHRISTMAS

*This arrangement offers a joyous welcome for Christmas house guests. The polished scales make an unusual container for the traditional yuletide greenery which is mixed with a little feathery fern, wild clematis and the filigree baubles.*

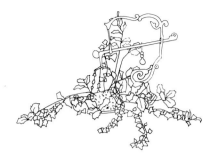

SIZE
99 cm × 53 cm (39 in × 21 in).

CONTAINER
French brass scales 48 cm (19 in) high, the
weighing pan 25 cm (10 in) in diameter.

EQUIPMENT
A block of well soaked foam 15 cm ×
15 cm × 9 cm (6 in × 6 in × 3½ in).

FOLIAGE
Fresh
  Asparagus plumosus (asparagus fern).
  Hedera helix 'Glacier' (ivy).
  Ilex aquifolium 'Argenteo-marginata'
  (holly), some leaves completely yellow.

SEEDHEADS
Glycerined
  Clematis vitalba (wild clematis, traveller's
  joy, old man's beard), gilded.

ACCESSORIES
Round and star-shaped, filigree, gold
baubles. Small gold baubles in clusters on
long wire stems.

ARRANGER
Pamela McNicol

*1* Place a support under the scale pan until the arrangement is completed, then it can be removed and the weight adjusted until the bar is horizontal. Form the outline with stems of the cream-leaved holly; use it low on both sides and with slightly shorter pieces out at the front and to the back. Add a well variegated stem up behind the scales towards the right and trails of the ivy low along the top of the chest as well as forwards and backwards across the chest. Remember as you work that this arrangement will be seen from all round.

*2* With shorter pieces of holly, work in towards the centre on both sides. Then take three curving stems of asparagus fern. Use two at the back—one on the right and the second on the left—and bring the third piece curling round on the left towards the front. Next add the gilded seedheads of the feathery wild clematis; these stems repeat and slightly emphasize the original outline.

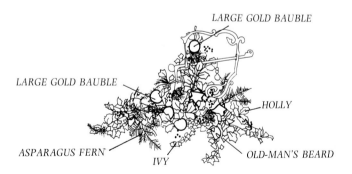

LARGE GOLD BAUBLE

LARGE GOLD BAUBLE

HOLLY

ASPARAGUS FERN

IVY

OLD-MAN'S BEARD

*3* Take the long stems of tiny gold baubles next and place these through the middle of the design and also out to join the tallest stem and those giving both width and depth. Finally add the larger baubles, one near the top of the scales and the others where they, too, will catch the light. Leave plenty of space between them. Balance the weight so that there is a little space between the arrangement and the chest and, having done this, the natural curves of the foliage will show more clearly.

# PASTEL COLOURS

*Among the fresh and the artificial foliage both fresh and dried flowers have been combined with charming results in this unusual Christmas decoration. The colours suggest mother-of-pearl and the matt black of the Victorian fireplace makes an excellent background for a design which could, so easily, be adapted for other special celebrations.*

*1* Tape the six dishes in place on their stands. Secure the largest dish in the fireplace opening, if necessary standing it on a block to bring it directly behind the decorative iron front. With the feathers and then the sprays of yew, suggest the shape of a Victorian fan inside the fire opening. Add pearlized leaves, some just in front of the feathers and a spray down on each side, with a little of the ruscus in front of the spray on the right. Add the teasel around the fan shape to complete the outline.

*2* Work next on the arrangements for the two stands. Place the candles and ribbon tails first, then add the yew, the ruscus, the pale blue artificial leaves and the gilded baubles on wire stems. Work with this material in a zig-zag way, up through all three arrangements on each stand. Add the teasels in the same way.

*3* Return to the central arrangement and complete it with the fresh flowers and the dried helichrysum. Keep the bronze-pink chrysanthemum towards the centre. Finish with a generous bow of separately wired loops and tails of the wider ribbon. Add the flowers to the stands. Group pale and darker chrysanthemums in each section. Then place cream helichrysums on both sides of these flowers in the two largest arrangements but just on the inner sides in the four small ones. There, too, finish the ribbon loop, this time the narrower width.

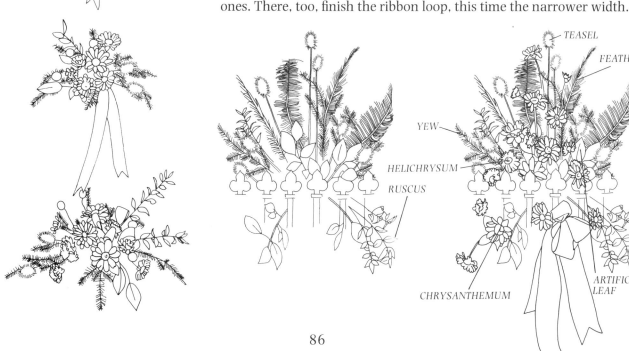

TEASEL

FEATHER

YEW

HELICHRYSUM

RUSCUS

CHRYSANTHEMUM

ARTIFICIAL LEAF

## SIZE
A pair of tiered arrangements, including candles, 112 cm × 38 cm (44 in × 15 in) at the base. A central arrangement, 38 cm × 51 cm (15 in × 20 in) (excluding ribbons).

## CONTAINERS
Two three-tier stands, painted matt black, each with three dishes, 6¼ cm (2½ in), 7½ cm (3 in), 10 cm (4 in) in diameter, also painted black. A dish 15 cm (6 in) in diameter.

## EQUIPMENT
Well-soaked squares of foam standing 4 cm (1½ in) above the rims of all seven dishes.

## FOLIAGE
Fresh
  *Taxus heterophylla* (yew), lightly sprayed with white paint.
  *Ruscus aculeatus* (butcher's broom), sprayed pearl pink.

## FLOWERS
Fresh
  Spray chrysanthemums, singles in pink and bronze-pink.
 Air dried
  *Helichrysum bracteatum* (strawflower, everlasting daisy), cream.

## SEEDHEADS
Air dried
  *Dipsacus fullonum* (teasel), sprayed pale pink.

## ACCESSORIES
Artificial leaves, turquoise-blue, pearl finish.
Baubles, small, golden.
Two candles, pale pink.
Feathers, pale pink.
Ribbons, pale pink, approximately 150 cm (5 ft) long and 5 cm (2 in) wide for tails and loops, and 3 metres (10 ft) long by 3 cm (1¼ in) wide.

*ARRANGER*  Beryl Gray.

# HELTER-SKELTER

*This 'whirly' tree is an idea which can be adapted for many party occasions.
It was designed for Thanksgiving or Christmas and, standing on the pine
table with the candles and the crackers, it makes an attractive decoration. It
could be used in the centre of a dining table and, by increasing or decreasing
the size, there is scope for using trees in many settings. See the list of ideas on
the facing page.*

*SIZE*
61 cm × 25 cm (24 in × 10 in).

*CONTAINER*
A mesh plant-pot holder, 10 cm (4 in) high
and 10 cm (4 in) across the top.

*EQUIPMENT*
A plastic plant-pot, 9 cm (3½ in) high and
9 cm (3½ in) across the top.
A slim bamboo cane, 56 cm (22 in) tall (this
must have a hollow stem at the top; keep
cutting until one appears and then trim to
the required length). Two metres (79 in) of
thin, flexible galvanized wire or green
garden wire, wound in a spiral like a snail
shell, but first make a hook at one end to fit
in the hole at the top of the cane. A few
pebbles for stability in the base of the plant-
pot. Household cement mixed to a fairly stiff
consistency (the plant-pot is filled to within
1½ cm (½ in) of the top, the bamboo cane is
put in the centre and checked for
straightness, and the household cement left
to harden). Narrow red ribbon (the type
with a decorative picot edge), 2½ metres,
(100 in), or more. A reel of grey-green
cotton. Glue. A bag of reindeer moss from
the florist.

*FLOWERS*
Dried while standing in a jar containing
1½ cm (½ in) water
   *Gypsophila paniculata* (baby's breath, chalk
   plant). Some left natural, some sprayed
   with green metallic-finish car paint and
   some with orange-red car paint.
Air dried
   *Helichrysum bracteatum* (strawflower,
   everlasting daisy).
   *Lagurus ovatus* (hare's-tail grass, rabbit's-
   tail grass). Dyed a pale golden colour
   when purchased.
   *Limonium sinuatum (Statice sinuatum)*
   (notch-leaf or winged statice).

*SEEDHEADS*
Air dried
   *Papaver somniferum* (opium poppy),
   sprayed with green metallic-finish car
   paint.

*ARRANGER*
Rose Marie Tree

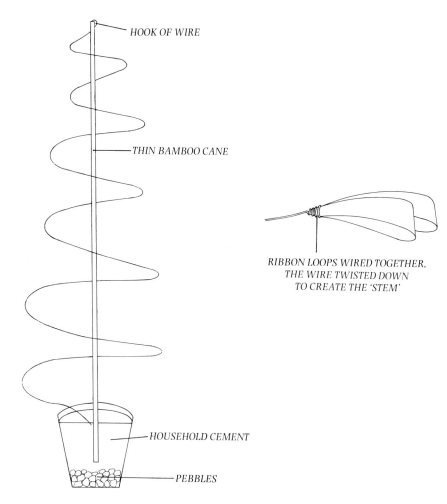

HOOK OF WIRE

THIN BAMBOO CANE

RIBBON LOOPS WIRED TOGETHER,
THE WIRE TWISTED DOWN
TO CREATE THE 'STEM'

HOUSEHOLD CEMENT

PEBBLES

**1** First dampen the moss to make it manageable and then glue on
small clumps all round the spiral; wind cotton thread over to
secure it. Start gluing the flowers and seedheads in place, keeping to
the same sequence—statice, helichrysum, gypsophila, poppy, hare's-
tail grass—finishing each time with a bow. End with a bow.

**2** Wind ribbon round the bamboo and glue neatly at each end.
Insert the hook of the spiral in the hole at the top of the cane.
Adjust the shape and insert two loops of ribbon, wired together, in the
top. Cover the cement in the flower-pot with moss and put it in the
container. If necessary, finish off with a few more bows.

Make one which is larger and stand it in a red flowerpot in the hall; surround it with the family's Christmas presents.

Make a set of tiny trees in golden shades and use one to mark each guest's place at a golden wedding celebration dinner.

Design a set of trees in several sizes and use them to decorate a buffet table.

These are just a few ideas but the secret of success will be in increasing or decreasing the scale of everything used, and then the visual balance will be pleasing.

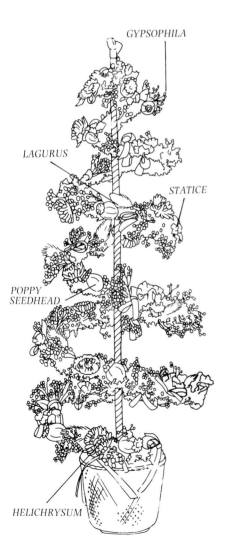

GYPSOPHILA

LAGURUS

STATICE

POPPY
SEEDHEAD

HELICHRYSUM

# PARTY CRACKERS

*The crackers can be made by following the instructions with the diagrams below. Size, colour, decoration and, of course, content, are all a matter of choice.*

## EQUIPMENT
Crêpe paper; lining paper; stiffening card; bangers; mottoes; gifts; glitter and paint; dried flowers; glue for attaching decorations; glue for sticking paper; needle and thread; cord; ribbon; net; tiny cones; pressed and artificial leaves and petals.

## ARRANGER
Mary Napper

## STAGE 1
*Crêpe paper, 29 cm × 16 cm (11½ in × 6¼ in).*
*Lining paper, 28 cm × 15 cm (11 in × 6 in).*
*Card, 15 cm × 9 cm (6 in × 3½ in).*
Lay the material out as shown. The grain of the crêpe paper must run lengthways. The short ends of the paper can be scalloped, and a band of gold or other coloured paper is stuck on the wrong side to show between the scallops. The join is covered with a short piece of ribbon.

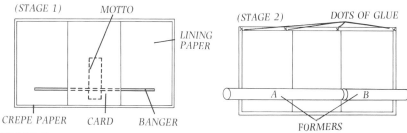

## STAGE 2
*Formers for crackers:*
*Former A—25 cm × 4 cm (10 in × 1½ in).*
*Former B—12½ cm × 4 cm (5 in × 1½ in).*
Roll the cracker round the formers, *away* from you. Roll tightly and stick firmly.

## STAGE 3
Lift to a horizontal position with your left hand, supporting Former B with thumb and first finger, the other fingers wrapped round A. Gently pull B out about 2 cm (¾ in) and take a piece of cord in your right hand, loop it round and pull gently to make a 'neck' between A and B. Unwind the cord, remove B and drop a gift into the cracker. Pull out A and wind the cord as for B. Release, secure the necks carefully and the cracker is ready for decoration.

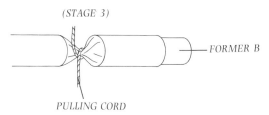

Build up a centre decoration by gluing on suitable materials; a band of decorative paper or ribbon can be added round the cracker first. Many other ideas can be tried.

### TO ADD FRILLS

*With net.* You will need four pieces of net for each cracker, 35½ cm × 15 cm (14 in × 6 in). Fold these in half lengthways, two for each end. Gather and tie in place firmly at the necks of the crackers. The edges can be decorated, perhaps with glitter.
*With crêpe paper.* Cut four pieces of the paper, 30½ cm × 7½ cm (12 in × 3 in) and scallop these along the long sides. Fold lengthways with the top layer two thirds the depth of the lower layer. Open the paper out again and gather along the crease line. Attach the frill to the neck of the cracker, the shorter side towards the middle. Take a length of lacy ribbon, 30½ cm (12 in) and gather before attaching over the crease in the paper frill. Fold the shorter length of paper back over the ribbon.

*1* The tallest stem of the arrangement is a carefully selected piece of the holly 'Aureo-marginata' and this is put in place first, its tip exactly above the centre of the container. Place further, shorter, stems of this holly on either side. Vary the lengths of the stems as you add more holly towards the middle, out to the right and down at the front. The outline is completed using the second, brighter holly on the left; there its stronger variegation and larger leaf will balance the stems on the right which sweep down towards the table. Now give depth to the design with the tree heath. Take three stems and use these towards the back, finishing about two-thirds of the way up and placing them so that their different texture will show amongst the glossy leaves. Take curving stems of the ivy out at both sides, close to the holly. Finish this stage of the design with three stems of the clear yellow holly leaves, high on the left, lower and in a little on the right and lower again on the left.

*SIZE*
127 cm × 84 cm (50 in × 33 in).

*CONTAINER*
A large polished pewter candlestick, 41 cm (16 in) high and 20 cm (8 in) across the base.

*EQUIPMENT*
A bowl, $16\frac{1}{2}$ cm ($6\frac{1}{2}$ in) in diameter and $7\frac{1}{2}$ cm (3 in) deep. A block of well-soaked foam cut to fit and standing $7\frac{1}{2}$ cm (3 in) above the rim, taped to the bowl and then to the candlestick.

*FOLIAGE*
Fresh
    *Asparagus plumosus* (asparagus fern).
    *Erica arborea* 'Alpina' (tree heath).
    *Hedera helix* 'Glacier' (ivy).
    *Ilex aquifolium* 'Aureo-marginata' (holly).
    *Ilex aquifolium* 'Lawsoniana' (holly).

*FLOWERS*
Fresh
    Carnations, florists' spray, pale orange.
    Lilies 'Mid-Century' hybrids,
    'Enchantment' and 'Tabasco'.

*SEEDHEADS*
Air dried
    *Papaver* (poppy), purchased, spray painted dull gold and dull red.
Glycerined
    *Clematis vitalba* (wild clematis, traveller's joy, old man's beard), lightly gilded.

*ARRANGER*
Pamela McNicol

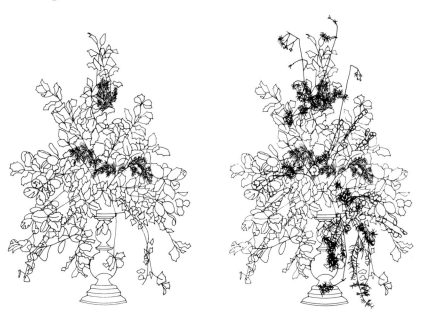

*2* Add the gilded clematis next. This feathery texture should be used first above and to both sides of the tallest stem, then bring some more through the centre in a slightly diagonal line towards the right. From the front bring another piece of the clematis forward and down and, alongside it, add a stem of asparagus fern to curl right down to the table at the right. With the spray carnations add soft colour out at both sides, high and low on the right and half-way up on the left; recess a few single blooms through the centre.

*3* Use both shades of the orange lilies next. Put the darker 'Tabasco' towards the middle and recess it a little, and place the lighter 'Enchantment' towards the outside. Take an almost fully-opened stem of this paler lily and give it pride of place in the heart of the arrangement, adding a spray of the bright yellow holly behind to give it added importance. Complete the design with the poppy seedheads, soft gold and dull red. They should be well spaced out in the arrangement and used to highlight the design, the highest just below the top. Only two, one out to the left and one to the right, are placed away from the centre.

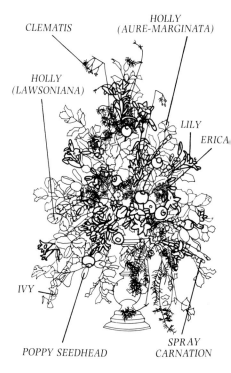

CLEMATIS

HOLLY (AURE-MARGINATA)

HOLLY (LAWSONIANA)

LILY

ERICA

IVY

POPPY SEEDHEAD

SPRAY CARNATION

# NOEL

*Traditional evergreens, fresh flowers and everlasting seedheads are mixed together and, in both the setting and the Christmas arrangement, there are many shapes and textures to enjoy. The angles and bright reflections of the brass candlesticks are repeated in the shining, spiny leaves of the holly while the quieter gleam of the pewter is suggested again by the painted curves of the poppy seedheads. Carved, plain and polished oak all play their part.*

# SILVER CHIMES

*The little figure appears to be enjoying the music from the glass bells in this
delightful variation on a Christmas tree theme. With no needles to fall it will
look just as charming at the end of the holiday as it does on Christmas Eve.
Here it stands on a table in a bedroom where the colour of the walls is picked
up in some of the bells and in the darker table cover.*

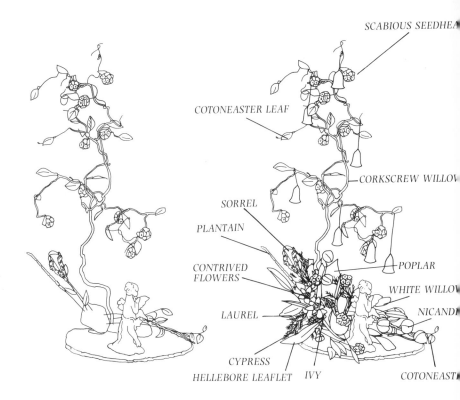

## SIZE
63½ cm × 43 cm (25 in × 17 in).

## EQUIPMENT
A small block of dried foam impaled on a
small but heavy pinholder. A very thin slice
of stone used as a base, 43 cm (17 in) across.
Cement-type filler mixed to a very stiff paste,
shaped to a roughly oval block, the salix
branch set in thus, and left to harden. Car
spray paint, silver. Glitter, silver and pink.
Glue. Thin wire.

## FOLIAGE
Glycerined
    *Chamaecyparis lawsoniana* (Lawson's
    cypress).
    *Cotoneaster franchetii.*
    *Hedera helix* (ivy).
    *Mahonia.*
    *Prunus laurocerasus* 'Otto Luyken' (laurel).
Pressed
    *Helleborus foetidus* (stinking hellebore),
    leaflets.
    *Populus candicans* 'Aurora' (balm of
    Gilead).

## SEEDHEADS
Air dried
    *Nicandra physaloides* (shoo-fly, apple of
    Peru), lightly sprayed silver.
    *Plantago major* (common or ratstail
    plantain).
    *Scabiosa stellata* 'Drumstick' (annual
    scabious), lightly tipped with silver.
    *Rumex acetosa* (sorrel).

## OTHER PLANT MATERIAL
Flower forms made from *Larix* (larch) cones
and small leaves from *Araucana araucana* (*A.
imbricaria*) (monkey puzzle, Chile pine).
(Method as described for made-up
(contrived) flowers on page 123.)
*Salix matsudana* 'Tortuosa' (corkscrew or
dragon's claw willow), branch.

## ACCESSORIES
Glass bells, glittered.

## ARRANGER
Jill Findlay

**1** Wire a few of the glycerined cotoneaster leaves on the salix
branch to look as natural as possible, then add some of the
scabious seedheads. Put the branch on the stone with the stem
coming up a little to the left of the middle and two-thirds back. Add the
pinholder with its block of foam on the left, just in front of the branch.
With stems of cotoneaster and plantain and sorrel seedheads, establish
the width of the arrangement, forward a little on the right and back
on the left. Put the little figure in place.

**2** Bring each stem out from the foam, remembering to include the
figure within the design. The nicandra is placed out to the right
and up to follow the line of the salix branch. The larger leaves, the
poplar, the laurel and the ivy, form a background and the laurel
especially strengthens the line out to the left. Curving hellebore
leaflets, contrived flowers and little sprays of the cypress add interesting
shapes and textures. Finish by tying the bells in place with fine wire or
cotton thread.

94

# HOGMANAY

*Ring out the old, ring in the new, a special arrangement for a New Year's Eve party. Fresh flowers for the coming year are mixed with fruits, feathers and leaves harvested in the old year. The colours are repeated in the Scottish Paisley shawl and the bells wait for the moment of celebration.*

**1** Place the platter so that one handle shows at the front of the design. Then put the plant saucer two-thirds of the way back and slightly to the right. Drape the shawl across the corner of the chest and round behind the saucer. Establish the height of the design with a tall and curving palm leaf. (Palm leaves can be coaxed into curves with your hands but it may be easier if they are slightly dampened and then tied, or pinned in position on a board, and left to dry.) Add two cycas leaves, low at the left, a little higher at the right. Place the straw fans on the left, the higher one turning in slightly towards the heart of the arrangement and the lower one turning in a little more. Add a magnolia leaf on the right above the cycas.

**2** Strengthen the design with two of the darker, glycerined palm leaves. These will have more importance if they are trimmed. Place the taller on the right of the curving palm and the shorter on the left and, at the back, use another slim and untrimmed leaf. Add the feathers next, the large orange ones across the design, low on the left, and higher and out to the back on the right. Place three pheasant-tail feathers on the left with one coming right down over the edge of the chest. Between the fans and the two higher feathers on the left, add a dried cycas leaf and complete this stage with a large, dark brown fatsia leaf to mask the foam and form a background for the flowers. Place the bells at the front on the right.

**3** Take the three stems of Chinese lanterns and with them repeat the orange of the feathers—high in the centre, as outline interest on the right, and a short stem low on the left. Add the painted grasses to strengthen the lines and accentuate the colours of the first and last of these stems. Now use the aspidistra leaves, one out over the right-hand fan and another to the left of the tallest palm leaf, its curve repeating the twist of the Chinese lantern stem. Place the gourds around the bells. Then put in the loofahs; one forward on the right, another behind the aspidistra leaf on the right, and the third between the fans on the left. Use the feathery chokes next, one above the bells, the other higher and slightly to the right. Then add the three large chrysanthemums to suggest a triangle with the chokes. Fill in the centre of this with spray chrysanthemums. Take a taller stem up to the left, another a little lower on the right and, finally, recess a few short flowers in above the bells.

*SIZE*
122 cm × 122 cm (48 in × 48 in).

*CONTAINER*
A flat wicker platter, 61 cm (24 in) in diameter.

*EQUIPMENT*
A shallow plastic plant saucer, 15 cm (6 in) in diameter, with a heavy pinholder anchoring a square of wet foam, this taped securely to the saucer.

*FOLIAGE*
Air dried
  *Cycas revoluta* (sago palm).
  *Phoenix canariensis* (canary date palm).
Glycerined
  *Aspidistra elatior* (cast-iron plant).
  *Fatsia japonica* (*Aralia sieboldii, A. japonica*) (false castor-oil plant, Japanese fatsia).
  *Magnolia grandiflora* (bull bay).

*FLOWERS*
Fresh
  Florists' chrysanthemums, three large yellow.
  Spray chrysanthemums, apricot-coloured, three stems.
Air dried
  *Cynara scolymus* (globe artichoke), two chokes.

*GRASS*
*Bromus macrostachys* (brome grass), air dried, painted orange.

*FRUITS*
*Cucurbita pepo* (ornamental gourd), three.
*Luffa cylindrica* (loofah), wired, three small.
*Physalis alkekengi* (Chinese lanterns, bladder cherry), three stems (air dried).

*ACCESSORIES*
Two straw fans, 35 cm (13½ in) across. Two hand bells. Feathers, two large, orange-dyed, and three pheasant.

*ARRANGER*
Bill Lomas

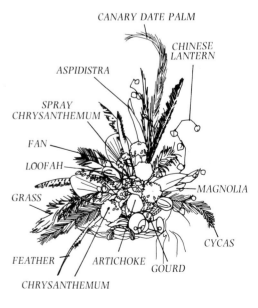

# TWELFTH NIGHT

*The decoration for a Twelfth Night party repeats many of the lovely colours in the Chinese wall covering. The fresh fruit and the daintiness of the garland with its companion trees make a welcome contrast to the evergreens which have decorated the home since Christmas Eve. Tomorrow all will go but tonight there is a party.*

*1* Construct the trees by first covering the pots with the blue velvet, carefully smoothing and gluing it in place. Turn the velvet over the tops of the pots and glue it down about $2\frac{1}{2}$ cm (1 in) below the rims. Next cover the central two-thirds of the canes with the silver-grey ribbon. Bind it round closely and glue the ends securely. Lay a circle of card over the holes in the pots before half filling with gravel. Over this put a layer of stiff cement mix to just below the velvet. Put the canes in place, absolutely upright and central with the unsharpened end sunk to the bottom of the pot. Cover the cement with the glass chippings. Either put the foam balls in place on the canes or work with them mounted on slimmer canes to be held in the hand. They must sit securely on the canes when they are finished, so do not widen or deepen the hole as you work.

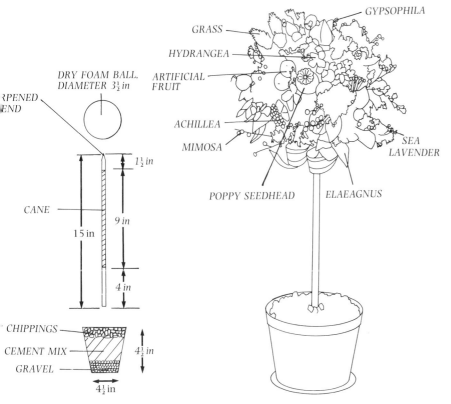

**GYPSOPHILA**
**GRASS**
**HYDRANGEA**
**ARTIFICIAL FRUIT**
**DRY FOAM BALL, DIAMETER 3½ in**
**RPENED END**
**ACHILLEA**
**MIMOSA**
**CANE**
**SEA LAVENDER**
**POPPY SEEDHEAD**
**ELAEAGNUS**
**15 in**
**1½ in**
**9 in**
**4 in**
**CHIPPINGS**
**CEMENT MIX**
**GRAVEL**
**4½ in**
**4½ in**

## SIZE

Overall width 76 cm (30 in). Garland with fruit 53 cm (21 in) across. Trees 45 cm (17½ in) high, 25½ cm (10 in) across the tops, 11½ cm (4½ in) across tubs.

## EQUIPMENT

A circle composed of 2½ cm chicken wire shaped and filled with dry foam and covered with kitchen foil (dull side out), 43 cm (17 in) in diameter.
Two balls of dry foam, 9 cm (3½ in) in diameter. Two flower pots, 11½ cm (4½ in) in diameter and 11½ cm (4½ in) high.
Two slim canes, 38 cm (15 in) long, the top ends sharpened for about 4 cm (1½ in). Blue velvet to cover the pots. Narrow silver-grey ribbon to cover the canes. Glue. A small quantity of gravel. Household cement. Glass chippings (broken car windscreen glass). Red ribbon for bows, 2 cm (¾ in) wide. Blue ribbon for bows, 2½ cm (1 in) wide. Plant pot saucer, 15 cm (6 in) in diameter. Two small pewter plates, 12½ cm (5 in) in diameter. Tissue paper.

## FOLIAGE

Air dried
  *Elaeagnus macrophylla* (oleaster), single leaves sprayed to deeper cream.

## FLOWERS

Air dried
  *Acacia dealbata* (mimosa).
  *Achillea filipendulina* (fern-leaved yarrow).
  *Alchemilla mollis*, sprayed silver.
  Florists' 'glixia' (star flower), purchased.
  *Gypsophila paniculata* (baby's breath, chalk plant), sprayed lime-green.
  *Helichrysum bracteatum* (strawflower, everlasting daisy).
  *Hydrangea macrophylla* (*H. hortensia, H. opuloides*) (common or French hydrangea), lightly sprayed blue, purple, soft orange.
  *Limonium latifolium* (broad-leaved statice, sea lavender), sprayed silver and glittered.

## GRASSES

Air dried
  *Phalaris arundinacea* (reed canary grass), a few sprayed pale orange.
  *Phragmites communis* (*Arundo phragmites*) (common reed).

## SEEDHEADS

Air dried
  Iris. Small cones.
  *Papaver somniferum* (opium poppy), glittered.

## FRUIT

Fresh
  Avocado, apples, grapes, kumquats, lychees, oranges and pineapple.
Dried
  Bell fruit, purchased.

## ACCESSORIES

Artificial small fruits, apples, cherries, limes, pears and strawberries.
Artificial leaves, plastic (lightly glittered) and fabric.

## ARRANGER  Joan Dunne

**2** Using similar material in the circle and the trees, work evenly round all three. Bring the content of the garland down to table level so that all the foil is covered. For the garland, use hydrangea heads mixed with elaeagnus and silk leaves, then add the fluffy reeds. Work next with all the flowers, varying the shapes, colours and textures. Next add the glittered leaves, cones, seedheads and a little canary grass. Finish the garland with groups of artificial fruit and a few small blue bows. Work on both trees together, keeping size and content similar. Start with the hydrangea heads, add achilleas and fill in with various leaves, sea lavender and gypsophila. Add the poppy heads and canary grass, and tuck in wired loops of red ribbon near the canes. Finish with groups of the artificial fruit and tiny bows of bright blue.

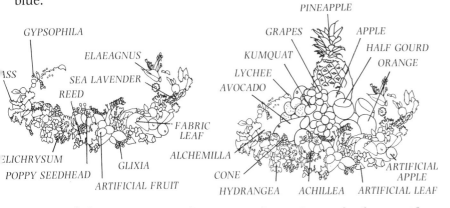

**GYPSOPHILA**
**ELAEAGNUS**
**SEA LAVENDER**
**REED**
**ASS**
**FABRIC LEAF**
**ELICHRYSUM**
**GLIXIA**
**ALCHEMILLA**
**POPPY SEEDHEAD**
**ARTIFICIAL FRUIT**
**PINEAPPLE**
**GRAPES**
**APPLE**
**KUMQUAT**
**HALF GOURD**
**LYCHEE**
**ORANGE**
**AVOCADO**
**CONE**
**ARTIFICIAL APPLE**
**HYDRANGEA**
**ACHILLEA**
**ARTIFICIAL LEAF**

**3** Stand the two trees on the pewter plates. Group the fruit inside the garland. Put the plant saucer, upturned, towards the back and to the right with crunched tissue paper around and over it. Place the pineapple on the saucer, angled to the right, then the larger fruit around, the grapes over this fruit in the middle, lychees and kumquats on the left and the bell fruit on the right.

# EQUIPMENT
# HARVESTING AND
# PRESERVING
# TECHNIQUES

# EQUIPMENT

Apart from a selection of vases and other containers, the flower arranger does need a store of equipment and details follow of those most often used. Towards the end of this list you will find information about equipment which will be especially helpful when working with everlastings.

Each of the illustrations in this book is accompanied by a list of the equipment used by the arranger and, from time to time, it may be helpful to refer to the information given here.

## PLASTIC FOAM

*Absorbent*
This, when used for fresh arrangements or when fresh and preserved materials are mixed, should be well soaked beforehand and always kept fully charged with water. It can be used dry for everlasting arrangements. Soft in texture and very light when dry, it may need weighting in some way as well as carefully taping to the container.

*Dry*
This special non-absorbent foam is firm in texture and generally useful for all everlasting arrangements except, perhaps, when using the most slender or fragile stems.

## PINHOLDERS (*Needlepoint holder*)
Pinholders are available in various sizes, weights and shapes. Some are designed for specific purposes. Those for placing under foam for anchorage or for securing branches are heavy and have the minimum of strong pins. Others have closely set pins for fine stems or are heavy with more widely set pins for large arrangements and thick stems. Choosing the right pinholder is important and will ensure that the arrangement has been provided with adequate balancing weight and stem anchorage.

## PUTTY SUBSTANCES
Putty-type material is used for fixing pinholders to containers and similar tasks. It is essential for both surfaces to be dry.

## CHICKEN-WIRE (*Wire-netting*)
There are two mesh sizes used most often. The larger, 5 cm (2 in), can serve as a basis for an arrangement. It is crunched up to fit the container, with some of the cut ends left at the top to hook over the rim. This sized mesh is more flexible and easier to handle than the smaller, $2\frac{1}{2}$ cm (1 in) kind but the smaller size can be shaped to fit over

a block of foam to prevent it disintegrating as an arrangement is built up. The larger mesh can be used in the same way but it will cut into the foam more when it is pulled in place and secured to the container. Chicken-wire can be used as a basis for shapes which are to be filled with moss or wet foam (see 'Evergreen' and 'Twelfth Night').

## TAPE

### Florists' tape
This tape, often purchased as *gutta percha*, is used for binding on and covering false stems and it can be used for sealing the ends of dried stems when they are to be mixed with fresh. It is made of a stretchy rubber substance and can lose its elasticity in store.

### Securing tape
A special tape is available for strapping foam or chicken-wire to containers, also containers to stands. It is used as for a parcel. The surfaces of the tape and whatever it is to adhere to must be absolutely dry.

### Cellulose tape
Both single and double-sided cellulose tape are useful and single is satisfactory for mending broken or cracked stems.

## CONES
Metal or plastic cones can be purchased in several sizes and are used when it is necessary to raise stems higher in an arrangement. The cones can be fixed directly in the foam or chicken wire or mounted on sticks and these placed in the foam or wire or on pinholders. Pressing the cone end on to pins directly will damage both the cone and the pinholder. Cones are filled with foam or wire and used either for fresh or dried material.

## WIRES

### Stub wire
Stub wires are used for strengthening or shaping stems or for creating false ones. They are also helpful for shaping material, for instance when taped in place at the back of a leaf which can then be curved. In some dried work they are used for attaching material to backgrounds. These wires are sold in bundles by weight. The higher the gauge the finer the wire. Lengths vary but a generally useful length is 260 mm (10 in). Silver stub wires are available for fine work.

### Reel wire
Wire sold on reels can be purchased in various finishes, the three most usual being coated in green, uncoated and silver. Reel wire is used for binding and securing in many ways and it is selected to be as unobtrusive as possible but strong enough for the chosen task.

## POLYTHENE
Thin polythene is used for covering wet foam to stop evaporation while still allowing stems to be pushed through into the foam. Medium weight polythene can be used when fresh flowers and foliage will be out of water for a length of time. They must be thoroughly charged with water before packing and completely enfolded, including the stem ends, then kept cool and dark. Polythene bags are often the

most suitable for this purpose but for very long stems sheets of this plastic can be used inside flower boxes. Heavy polythene makes a satisfactory work sheet but if it is used on the floor and it gets wet it can be slippery.

## CUTTING TOOLS
Secateurs, sharp knife, scissors and wire-cutters.

## WATER CONTAINERS
Buckets, preferably with side handles for ease of carrying and to avoid damage to the contents.

Spray, with a fine nozzle, for refreshing arrangements.

Watering-can, small and with a long spout for topping-up arrangements.

## HAIR LACQUER
Lacquer can be sprayed over seedheads which have a tendency to 'blow' in a warm, dry atmosphere—pampas and reed mace for instance.

## EXTRA EQUIPMENT FOR WORKING WITH PRESSED EVERLASTINGS AND ON PLAQUES, CONES AND CIRCLES

## FLOWER PRESSES
These can be purchased in several sizes from the small pocket size upwards, or they can be made at home. You will need two outer plywood or hardboard squares, sheets of cardboard cut to match and sheets of blotting paper of the same size. The pressure is put on the press by fixing corner wing nuts and these are turned to give equal pressure at all four corners. Two pieces of blotting paper are put between the sheets of card and then material for pressing put between them. Alternatively, heavy books, such as old telephone directories, can be used with blotting paper or tissues between the leaves. They should be stacked with more weight on top. Identifying labels should be fixed to the places where material is being pressed to avoid unnecessary movement.

## ADHESIVES
Various types of glues and gums are used and most arrangers have their favourites. For heavy material, a strong adhesive is necessary and the type used for floor tiles is satisfactory. Non-trailing types are most suitable for pictures where there is a fabric background or where there is a design with much of the background left clear; the decoration on page 26 is an example. Reasonably quick drying properties are helpful but the very rapidly drying types are not suitable.

## VARNISH
Nail-varnish or similar varnishes can be used to protect the ends of dried stems and for other effects such as a slight gloss. A nail-varnish remover is helpful when working with adhesives.

## CUTTING AND HANDLING TOOLS

Scissors—a selection for cutting stems, fabric, paper and card. A small pair with fine points is needed for small work.

Knives—a selection suitable for cutting backgrounds, mounts and heavy stems.

Nail file and a pair of pointed tweezers for handling delicate petals, etc.

Cocktail sticks, toothpicks or a finely pointed knitting needle for applying adhesives.

Magnifying glass.

# GROWING AND HARVESTING

If we consider the harvest from the garden and the additional supply which can be purchased from one source or another it becomes clear just how vast is the choice of flowers, leaves, branches, seedheads, fruits, fungus and driftwood from which we may design our long-lasting arrangements.

A seeing-eye is essential when making our selection and it is necessary to have patience and a willingness to try things out and to accept the occasional failure. Sometimes lack of success is because the time of picking was not right or the conditions in which it was treated and stored were not satisfactory. In this book we can share the experience of others and so avoid some of the disappointments. Here we consider some of the plants which can be grown or bought and how to preserve them.

## GROWING EVERLASTINGS

### Annuals and biennials

There are many annuals which can be grown specifically for drying; they are varied in shape, colour and size but usually papery in texture. If space is available it is possible to include these annuals in the yearly plan for the garden, perhaps trying a new kind each year to go with the already established favourites.

In general they do best in full sun and poor soil but with adequate moisture for good germination and early growth. Too much richness of diet, low sunlight and late summer wetness all contribute to leggy growth and poor flowering.

A short list follows. All should be air dried unless otherwise stated.

### Daisy forms

*Ammobium alatum* (sandflower, winged everlasting), silvery-white with yellow centres.
*Helichrysum bracteatum* (strawflower, everlasting daisy), wide selection of colours from cream to bright red and with many yellows and oranges.
*Helipterum roseum (Acrinoclinium roseum)*, both in the white to pink range.
*Rhodanthe manglesii (Helipterum manglesii)*.
*Xeranthemum annuum* (immortelle), white to a purplish-pink.

### Tall stems

*Atriplex hortensis* (mountain spinach, orache). 'Rubra' is the red form which grows to 183 cm (6 ft) or more. There is a green form which is desirable but hard to find.

*Delphinium consolida* (larkspur), blue, purple, pink or white, 'Giant Imperial' strain 1.2 m (4 ft).

*Digitalis purpurea* (common foxglove), and other foxglove species, all the seedheads will air dry but are more satisfactory glycerined, when they turn a mid-brown and are less brittle.

*Molucella laevis* (bells of Ireland), green bracts turn a parchment colour when air dried and a richer cream when treated with glycerine but they can then be bleached to a paler colour in sunlight. Germination is aided by over-night soaking in warmth before sowing and a temperature of around 60°F is required. Half-hardy.

*Verbascum bombyciferum (V. broussa)* and other varieties (mullein), 1.5 m (5–6 ft) or more, woolly grey stems with seedheads.

### Cascading forms

*Amaranthus caudatus* (love-lies-bleeding, tassel-flower), half-hardy, red and green forms with long drooping stems of tiny, close-set flowers.

*Humulus japonicus (H. scandens)* (hop), twisting vine with papery bracts in clusters. It is most attractive if picked and dried when mature but still green. Apart from air-drying this will glycerine.

### Round forms

*Gomphrena globosa* (globe amaranth), flowers $2\frac{1}{2}$ cm (1 in) across, purple, red, pink, white or yellow, papery texture.

*Nicandra physalloides* (shoo-fly plant, apple of Peru), grown for its green calyx which has a tiny, apple-like fruit inside. The calyx dries to a parchment colour.

*Nigella damascena* (love-in-a-mist), seedheads have interesting 'feathers' and lines and vary in colour from pale green to brownish-purple.

*Papaver rhoeas* and

*Papaver somniferum* (poppies), both species have interesting seedheads which dry to grey shades.

*Scabiosa stellata* (drumstick scabious), an annual grown for its spherical seedheads which dry to a light beige, $2\frac{1}{2}$ cm (1 in) across.

### Various other shapes

*Cucurbita pepo ovifera* (ornamental gourds), half-hardy, ranging in size up to approximately 15 cm (6 in), in various colours and textures.

*Gypsophila elegans* (baby's breath), white or pink, sprays of tiny flowers.

*Limonium sinuatum* (notch-leaf or winged statice), angular stems and small flowers in clusters. Mixed colours including blue, pink, purple, yellow and white.

*Lunaria annua* (satin flower, moonwort, money plant, honesty), has useful seedheads which are disc-shaped with greenish-purple outer cases and silvery inside.

*Zea mays* (ornamental maize), grown for its mahogany-red, strawberry-shaped cobs, 4 cm ($1\frac{1}{4}$ in) long, also, long cobs of mixed colours—yellow, red, orange and purple tones, about 12 cm (4–5 in) long.

### Grasses

*Agrostis nebulosa* (cloud grass), a dainty grass giving a hazy effect.

*Briza maxima* and *Briza minor* (greater and lesser quaking grass), spikelets which dry to a cream colour.

*Hordeum jubatum* (squirrel-tail grass), can be grown as a perennial as well as an annual. Curving heads up to 8 cm (3 in) long, with closely set, slender awns.

*Lagurus ovatus* (hare's-tail grass), soft, densely hairy white seedheads, $3\frac{1}{2}$ cm ($1\frac{1}{2}$ in) long.

*Rhynchelytrum roseum (Tricholaena rosea)* (wine grass), long, purplish-red, silky inflorescences which fade to pink and silver.

All the annuals and biennials listed above appear in comprehensive seed catalogues but there are many more to try.

## HARVESTING FROM THE ESTABLISHED GARDEN

It can be rewarding to gather from many of the herbaceous perennials and other plants in the garden and to add them to the stock of everlastings ready for use in the home. All will have been planted for their own special seasonal displays but many have attractive flowers or seedheads which will dry satisfactorily.

Some of the spring bulbs have lovely seedpods. The bluebell *(Endymion hispanicus)*, the grape hyacinth *(Muscaris botryoides)* and some of the tulips, especially the smaller species, for instance *Tulipa tarda* and *T. turkestanica*, both flower generously with several blooms to a stem and have elegant little seedpods 3 cm (1 in) or so long in clusters. A little larger is the lady tulip, *T. clusiana*, with its single seedhead. All these dry to cream and parchment shades.

The seedheads of wallflowers *(Cheiranthus* and *Erysimum)* will take up a glycerine solution and so turn a rather darker brown than when they are air dried. The solution stops the pods splitting and scattering the seeds—but perhaps those empty, twisting pods would be just right for a particular design, and the store cupboard should hold a few of each.

Here, then, is the springtime starting point for a collection. Summer's delphiniums, peonies and many of the earlier flowering summer irises are just three kinds of herbaceous plants which have interesting seedheads and there are many flowers which air dry well. For a store of pressed material the choice is even wider. A brief list follows of plants which are easy to grow and air dry satisfactorily.

*Achillea*
(The yarrow family.) The species range from dwarf kinds to *Achillea filipendulina* which grows to 1.2 m (4 ft). There are yellow, pink and white varieties. All have flat heads which are composed of tiny flowers and are good for cutting. All prefer hot and dry growing conditions.

*Anaphalis*
(Pearly everlasting.) The bunched heads of small white flowers have yellow eyes. When dry, the fluffy centres are attractive but tend to blow; when removed a disc of pale cream will be seen. *A. triplinervis* grows to 40 cm (16 in) and *A. yedoensis* is slightly taller. Plants prefer some moisture in the growing season and dryness in the winter.

*Artemisia*
(Western mugwort, white sage, cudweed are the familiar names for *A. ludoviciana*.) This is one example of the family which can be air dried. The long stems of silvery leaves and tiny flower buds are best picked before the flowers open. Grow in poor soil where it will reach 1.2 m (4 ft).

*Eryngium*
(Sea holly types.) The thistle-like, cone-shaped flower heads are surrounded by bracts. The flower heads of the various species range in

colour from grey and greenish blue to purplish-blue, drying to muted versions of these colours. The head of *Eryngium giganteum* are 5 cm (2 in) long; those of *E. amethystinum* are just $1\frac{1}{2}$ cm ($\frac{1}{2}$ in). *E. alpinum* has feathery bracts with metallic blue, 3 cm ($1\frac{1}{4}$ in) heads. The plants grow better on poorish soil and will tolerate drought.

*Lavendula*
(Lavender.) Spikes of well perfumed flowers in a variety of blue, purple and pink shades; white is also available. Pick before flowers are fully developed. Ideal conditions are light, well-drained soil and sunshine.

*Liatris*
(Blazing star, Kansas feather.) Tuberous rooted. *L. spicata* grows to 1 m (3 ft) and is available in white or mauve-pinks. This species will tolerate wetter conditions than some others.

*Stachys*
*Stachys grandiflora (S. macrantha)* (betony, woundwort) grows to 60–90 cm (2–3 ft) and develops useful seedheads. *S. lanata (S. byzantina, S. olympica)* (woolly betony, lamb's ears, lamb's tongue) throws up flower spikes of 30–40 cm ($1$–$1\frac{1}{2}$ ft) and the grey-leaved stems have tiny mauve flowers in clusters. Best picked before the buds show colour. These species are easily grown and tolerate some drought.

*Echinops*
(Globe thistle.) Globular heads which are spiky and a metallic blue on stems of 1.2 m (4 ft) or more. Pick before the flowers are fully open and dry quickly, otherwise they may shatter. Ultra-hardy and tolerates poor soil and drought.

The above list gives a variety of shapes, colours, sizes and textures and from this start many more garden plants will suggest themselves.

Leaves can be treated with glycerine solution (see page 112). Sprays of beech, *Fagus sylvatica*, in its various forms and colours and the white poplar, *Populus alba*, are examples which will absorb glycerine solution quite readily. The beech takes on a range of shades from pale chestnut to a blackish-brown depending on the time of picking and the variety; the earlier in the summer the paler the result for green beech. The poplar leaves turn dark brown on top but remain silver-grey beneath. Of the shrubs two examples which are very successful and useful in small arrangements are the common box, *Buxus sempervirens*, and *Pittosporum tenuifolium*.

As summer ends it is followed by the rich colours of autumn and many leaves can be pressed to preserve their brightness. More and more seedheads can be hung in bunches or stood in containers to air dry. Ferns can be pressed, adding useful green shades to the store, and bracken will give the same delicate fronds in golden tones.

The mop-head hydrangeas, *Hydrangea macrophylla (H. hortensis)*, turn colour and become papery with the first frosts and these large, rounded heads are very useful. The kitchen garden will produce more for the harvest. There may be leek seedheads, round and silvery-grey, like many others from that useful *Allium* family. Artichokes can be dried with their fluffy chokes or with these removed giving two very different shapes and textures. Parsley seedheads can be air dried and segments of the leaves, especially the less curly French varieties, press attractively. If radishes have been left to seed you will find little bunches of seedpods, each about 4 cm ($1\frac{1}{2}$ in) long.

Even in winter there can be much to gather: cones, acorns and their cups, beech cupules and interesting branches. All may have been brought down by high winds or hidden, perhaps, under lush growth earlier in the year. Driftwood, too, is part of the harvest and a walk along the shore after high seas or where a river has been in full spate may reveal treasure.

*THE HARVEST FROM THE FLORIST*

Nowadays good florists offer a continually increasing variety of ready-dried plant material. More and more opportunities occur for adding variety to our arrangements from this fascinating international exchange. Much of the florists' preserved material has been air dried. Some is bleached, much is lightly tinted with colour and some is heavily coloured. Freeze drying is another commercial method and, recently, material has become available which has been, to use the trade description, 'mummified', an unattractive name but the results are interesting and examples are included in the cover arrangement. Material from hot and dry climates is often bolder and firmer in texture than the plants grown in cooler climates. For instance, there are large curving spathes, protea flowers of many sizes and shapes, and interesting seedheads and grasses.

Anything which comes from a dry climate should be easy to look after if it is kept in similar conditions. Most dry off without difficulty but it is worth considering the glycerine method of preserving with some of the foliage and bracts. Eucalyptus is an example of the type of leaf which will absorb the solution easily and attractively, turning the colour from grey to mauve. *Molucella laevis* (bells of Ireland) bracts turn a lovely cream. It is worth looking for similar textures in less well-known items sold at the florists.

Flowers, such as larkspur, can be bought in bunches, ready dried or fresh. If fresh flowers are wanted for drying, try to buy them when they are just coming to the fully open stage, then dry them off speedily. Flowers which have been standing in water for any length of time will take longer and should be watched carefully for mould, especially at the stem ends. Gypsophila can be treated similarly and many other flowers will be worth experimenting with. Helichrysum, statice and grasses should be trouble free.

*Ruscus aculeatus* (butcher's broom) is another readily available florist's foliage. It will absorb the glycerine solution, taking on a good brown colour but it may take longer than eucalyptus to do so as it is thicker and more leathery. Variety of colour can be added by standing some in a sunny window after it has been treated. It will bleach to a paler colour, as will many of the tougher leaves and bracts.

Experience will help when deciding which flowers, leaves or seedheads to take home to air dry, to glycerine or to press. There may be some which will be successful when dried with desiccants or even in the microwave oven. The feel of the leaf, knowledge of its lasting qualities and the speed with which it is likely to absorb a solution or become dry, and the paperiness of a flower or a bract, all these will be reliable guides to the likelihood of success. Very fleshy flowers and leaves may be too full of moisture to be good subjects and fragile petals can bruise easily.

# PRESERVING PLANT MATERIAL

Today's homes and many other places where we may be invited to arrange flowers have a dry atmosphere, especially in the months when heating is high or air conditioning switched on. Here everlastings are especially useful and attractive.

It is pleasing to know that the main ingredients for success are enthusiasm and time, with expense being relatively low—in some cases minimal. Of the methods described here, air drying will provide a very large selection to choose from and will cost very little, perhaps nothing at all. Glycerine is expensive but everything which is successfully treated with this solution will be long-lasting and supple rather than brittle. If a large stock of glycerined material is needed it will be sensible to buy in bulk rather than in small bottles. Some desiccants are expensive but they can be re-used. For pressing it may be desirable to have flower presses; they can be either bought or made at home. Details are given on page 113.

The satisfaction of using home preserved everlastings is increased when experiments with material or methods prove successful and opportunities for changing our arrangements are just as frequent with these well-tempered materials as with fresh flowers and leaves. Whichever we are using, the real joy is in creating arrangements which add appropriate colour and interest to their settings.

## METHODS
Some plants dry best if they are arranged in shallow water and left in a dry but not too warm place, hydrangea heads for example. These should be gathered when they start to feel crisp to the touch; they will dry satisfactorily if picked earlier but the colour interest will be less. When they are completely dry they will be quite papery. An example of hydrangeas chosen for this purpose can be seen in 'Picked to Keep'.

## AIR DRYING
Material for drying by this method should be just coming to maturity, not too young, when the stems will tend to be rather limp, or too old, when the tendency may be for the flowers to fall apart. All plant material should be picked during a dry spell of weather. Air drying can be used for some leaves but most shrivel and become unattractive. Heavy textured leaves, such as those of aspidistra, strelitzia and hosta, take on interesting curves as they dry but leaving them in shallow water, as for the hydrangea heads, is likely to be more satisfactory, especially for the hosta leaves.

1 Deal with plant material as soon as it has been picked.
2 Strip surplus leaves off stems before bunching and tying together.

3 Bunch in fairly small quantities to avoid damaging the flowers.
4 Stems shrink as they dry so tie them up fairly tightly and check the bunches after a few days.
5 Hang the bunches up, heads downwards, in an airy, dry and, if possible, dark place. This ensures speedy drying and keeping a good colour.

## GLYCERINE METHOD

Again the plant material should be picked when it is coming to maturity, and during a dry spell of weather. Old or wet plant material will take up the solution more slowly and there will be a tendency for mildew to form. Cut ends dry out quickly so pick and then deal with a few stems at a time. Leaves which have taken on their autumn colours cannot be preserved by this method. Glycerined material is much more supple to use than air dried stems.

1 Make up a glycerine mixture using one third of glycerine to two thirds of boiling water.
2 Stir thoroughly and use at once.
3 Fill fairly narrow jars to a depth of about 8 cm (3 in).
4 Place the newly cut stems, a few to a jar. This way they should drink the solution quickly. Too many stems in one jar may mean there is not enough solution and the plant material shrivels before this is noticed. Too many stems can also result in crushed and unattractive results.
5 Stems will take up the solution if it is cold when they are put in, but the process will be slower.
6 Stand the jars in a dry, airy place, out of strong light.
7 The length of time taken by various kinds of plant material differs, but it is ready when it has taken on an interesting colour and is very slightly oily to the touch. A few days will be long enough for some material, two to three weeks for beech leaves, and much longer for heavy textured leaves such as those of aspidistra. Wipe over heavy leaves with the mixture as soon as they are picked to prevent them from drying out before they have taken up the solution. Some small, leathery leaves can be submerged until they are preserved.
8 Any solution which is left can be re-used.
9 Bleached effects can be achieved by standing the newly preserved material in a sunny window for a few days.
10 Dry storage is essential. This material can be packed in boxes ready for use.
11 Dusty and tired arrangements give no pleasure but glycerined material can be refreshed by being wiped over with a soapy cloth and then dried carefully. Steaming for a few seconds will allow a little re-shaping but, again, it must be dried well before being used or stored.
12 When preserved material is used with fresh, the ends of the preserved stems should be dipped into something which will waterproof them, such as varnish.

## DESICCANTS

Several types of desiccants can be used for preserving flowers, and leaves can also be treated in this way. Their purpose is to absorb moisture as quickly as possible and to leave a completely dry but brightly coloured flower which will hold its petals exactly as it did when it was picked.

Some desiccants are of a coarser grain than others. Sand is the heaviest and this must be washed and dried several times before it is used to remove impurities. Silica gel is less coarse and alum is finer. Borax is very fine and light; it does tend to clog on the petals but a mixture of sand and borax can be useful. The size and texture of the flower will suggest which will be the most suitable. The more delicate the flower the lighter the desiccant needed. After use, the desiccant must be thoroughly dried before it can be used again.

For this method airtight containers are necessary, their size and depth depending on the plant material to be dried in this way.

1 Put a layer of desiccant in the container to a depth of about 3 cm (1 in).
2 Place the bloom on top (no stem left on) and cover very carefully with desiccant, teasing it into every space between the petals so that each one is fully supported.
3 Add more desiccant to a depth of a further 2 cm ($\frac{3}{4}$ in).
4 Close and seal the container and leave it for a few days before examining. The flower should be dry and papery, if not it must go back in the desiccant for a little longer. If left too long it will become very fragile.
5 Dry and careful storage is essential.

## PRESSING

A specially made flower press is helpful but not essential. As an alternative, sheets of blotting paper can be used on either side of the material to be pressed, and these are then placed inside heavy books, such as obsolete telephone directories. This can be a completely satisfactory method but sufficient weight must be placed on top. Use markers to show what is being pressed and exactly where it is and then it will not be necessary to disturb the rest of the contents.

The most successful material for pressing is thin in texture and, of course, it should be dry when picked.

1 Remove the stems and, if required, press them separately.
2 Press single petals rather than whole flowers if they are bulky.
3 Include leaves of many shapes and sizes, tendrils and grasses.
4 Use sufficient weight to force the moisture out into the blotting paper quickly. The more fleshy subjects may need checking and moving to fresh blotting paper frequently.
5 Large flat leaves, such as aspidistra or ferns, can be pressed with a cool iron, placing them between sheets of blotting paper or newspaper first. This starts the drying process quickly. Afterwards they should be put under heavy weights.

Some flowers and leaves dry out quickly but their colours will hold better if they are left in the press for a long period; six months is not too long.

There are a few plants which can be treated in more than one way and a good example is the aspidistra. Leaves from this well known house-plant are long lasting when green. They will air dry, keeping their shape quite well and turning a mid-brown. They will also absorb the glycerine solution and go rather richer in colour and have a useful suppleness. They can be pressed also, but with this process they become a pale brown and are, naturally, flattened. So aspidistra leaves can provide a selection of shades of brown and some variety of form.

Following all this effort and time devoted to preserving and assembling a varied and interesting collection of everlastings, it is sensible to look after the material carefully. Suggestions on storage are given in the section that follows.

# STORAGE

It is essential for preserved material to be handled with care from the moment it is purchased or picked until it is brought out of store to be used.

The three most important things to consider when deciding on a suitable storage place are: a dry atmosphere, preferably very airy; adequate space; appropriate equipment for looking after both fragile and heavy material.

Damp should be recognized as the top priority problem but there are other dangers. It is surprising how much damage can be done by insects and spiders. Mice should not be overlooked; they will appreciate your harvest for both bed and board.

Do not be tempted to pick or buy more than you have sufficient storage space for; the results from overcrowding of fragile and often brittle material are not attractive.

## AIR DRIED AND GLYCERINED MATERIAL
Do not keep differently preserved materials together, though similar methods of storage will be satisfactory.

Storing in plastic bags or between sheets of polythene is unwise; the slightest damp will quickly result in mould.

Separate the various kinds of material. As soon as they are thoroughly preserved store carefully to prevent deterioration. If there is not a great deal of one type it may be possible to store it with another of similar weight but different appearance. For instance, poppy seedheads stored with iris pods can be quickly and easily separated and will not damage each other. Gypsophila and alchemilla heads would, on the other hand, become enmeshed and spoilt.

Strong cardboard boxes make good storage containers and flower boxes are ideal for long stems. Support separate layers with lightly crushed paper as you fill them, label the ends of the boxes clearly and stack so that these labels can be read and, when required, the necessary material can be traced and removed with the least possible disturbance.

Individual stems with large heads, such as *Allium giganteum* or *Hydrangea macrophylla*, can be packed in boxes, but the heads will need support similar to that which is given to large blooms packed for the florist. It is important to start at the bottom of the box with deep support for the first row of heads (rolled paper will do). Lifting the heads prevents them being flattened on one side. Supporting canes or thinner rolls of paper should be used between rows as the box is filled.

To protect very delicate material, bunch it carefully and then wrap it in paper (not a stiff paper as this will damage petals and leaves). Tie the bunches securely—soft string or soft twine will be suitable—and hang them up heads down. If bunches are to be stored in boxes, secure the wrapping with elastic bands, staples or sticky tape.

Many seedheads cast their seeds as they dry. To prevent this being a nuisance, a paper bag can be tied in place loosely over the heads of the bunches.

If there is sufficient space for hanging all the bunches in an airy, dry, dark place, this will be very satisfactory. They will be protected from dust if they are wrapped and, if the storage place is light, this covering will stop the fading of colours.

Bunches can be hung from the ceiling or from a specially constructed framework at a lower and more convenient level.

One other drying method is to use chicken wire stretched across a frame; $2\frac{1}{4}$ cm (1 in) mesh will be suitable for a wide variety of material, the individual stems being dropped through so that the heads are supported on the wire. Working from a stock stored on an open framework or hung from the ceiling is pleasant as everything can be seen and quickly selected.

## PRESSED MATERIAL

If possible leave pressed material in the flower press (or whatever has been chosen for pressing) for six months or longer. The colours will fade less readily when they are used and also it will be safe storage. Strong light will fade all dried material.

Allocate air-tight containers to each type of material and move the fragile petals, leaves, tendrils and stems with tweezers or a nail file. For tiny material, quite small boxes or tins will do but it is a good idea to use thin paper between layers as each box is filled. The less these little pieces are handled the more immaculate they will be. Larger pressed material, for instance ferns, will need more space but a large number can be packed in one box by layering between paper or card in the same way.

Damp-proof containers are essential unless the store is very dry. Clear labelling will save time and reduce the handling of the stock.

## DESICCANT-DRIED

Anything which has been dried by the desiccant method will be very fragile and it will re-absorb moisture rapidly. Great attention must be paid to its storage and to handling it in a dry atmosphere.

It is wise to add a sprinkling of the desiccant to the air-tight box or tin before it is sealed for storage, which is best done with adhesive tape if there is any chance of damp.

Different types of material should be stored separately and for the larger and many-petalled flowers, roses for instance, a carefully arranged support of soft tissue will help.

Do not be tempted to leave anything in the dessicant after the drying period; it will disintegrate very quickly.

Although this type of preserved material is so fragile, the results are attractive and 'Medley' is an example of one way in which it can be enjoyed.

## SEEDS

'Emily's Sampler' and 'Jacobean' are two examples of collages in which seeds have been used. There is a tremendous selection to choose from.

For ease of working, store each kind of seed in a separate container. See-through boxes are a great help and the enthusiast may find a small storage unit of the kind intended for nails, screws and so on, ideal.

Moisture should not be a problem with seeds purchased from the grocer, delicatessen or seed merchant, but when collecting from outdoors choose a dry day and do not add anything to your store until you are sure it is completely dry.

# FLOWERS AS GIFTS

It is a pleasant tradition to express our feelings and our friendship with flowers but if they are given after we have turned them into special and appropriate gifts, they can mean so much more.

Many of the designs in this book would make delightful presents. The smallest are, perhaps, the simplest to think of giving. However, there may be occasions for arranging flowers when you will take everything you need into someone else's home, or to a hotel or a church, and spend time there; then the flowers and your time and skill all become part of the giving.

The little posy of everlastings in 'Mother's Day' or the 'Gift of Flowers', where fresh and everlastings have been mixed together, are just two examples of small arrangements designed as gifts.

The simplicity suggested in 'The Summer Border', with its white background and clear colours, is suitable for a quite different setting from the two examples in 'Nostalgia' where one is a detailed and lovingly constructed picture suggested by a Victorian postcard and the other a set of tiny posies made into a small wall hanging.

When thinking of making and giving pictures, the mounting, framing and glazing all need careful attention if they are to suit both the picture and the place where they are to hang. With plaques, the background fabrics are especially important. 'Jacobean' and 'One of a Pair' are examples; here you can see how the fabrics, as well as the plants, play their part in the success of the design.

Gifts may be for a church. The Bible-marker in 'The Lectern' is one instance. Also, the large arrangement, 'Noel', is in a style which could so easily be used in a church at Christmas.

Perhaps the jar of flower heads and pot-pourri would make a welcome gift from a house guest. The paperweight and the decorated hat might please a teenage daughter.

A busy hostess may welcome a Thanksgiving or Christmas decoration rather than a bunch of flowers requiring her immediate attention. A generous selection of preserved flowers, leaves and seedheads, such as are seen in 'A Winter Evening', or, in very different style, 'Gleanings', could be chosen carefully and given to any enthusiastic arranger.

Finding something suitable to use as a container when giving an arrangement away is not difficult. Inexpensive plastic dishes with their fitting blocks of dry foam are a starting point. At the other end of the scale, a lovely container may be the real present and the flowers a temporary addition. In between comes a range of modestly priced items, and the arranger's ingenuity will play its part. Baskets are readily available and look attractive with most everlasting material;

118

they can be found in an almost unending variety of styles, colours and sizes. The problem of using inner dishes is not very likely to be important with dried flowers. In 'Colour Impact', a pale basket has been used to great effect. It has a shallow plastic dish holding the foam but this is more to stop little bits from falling through the wicker than for any other reason.

Giving long-lasting flowers, whether in bunches, arrangements or turned into keepsakes, means thinking very carefully about the possible setting if the gift is to give true pleasure.

# BOWS AND FANTASY FRUITS AND FLOWERS

During the winter months there are days of celebration when it is cheering and appropriate to add unexpected colours, a little sparkle and even some fantasy to our flowers—something we would not do at other seasons of the year.

There is much artificial material available to buy for our festive arrangements but in this book very little will be found. Instead there are designs which include the arrangers' own made-up (contrived) flowers, leaves or fruits. In every case these have been created from stocks of harvested plants, and some examples with instructions for making them follow. But first, a few hints on false stems and bows.

*FALSE STEMS*
Using wire.

*Cones*
Add stems when cones
are dry and fully open

In some cases wires can only be attached by drilling holes first; this may be necessary with hard or heavy materials.

False stems can be given to leaves. Small leaves can be wired individually and then attached to branches (see 'Silver Chimes') or made into sprays (see 'Winter Evening'). Each leaf can be fixed to thin wire with a small piece of adhesive tape or by 'stitching' the wire

120

through the leaf near the stem end. Larger leaves, for instance *Fatsia japonica* or *Aspidistra elatior*, will be easy to handle and mould into shape if they are given heavier gauge wire stems held in place at the back with a length of adhesive tape.

*Strawflowers*
Add stems when freshly
picked and soft

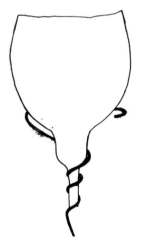

*Flowers with capsules*
Add stems when dry unless
very woody, then when
picked

Where wire stems will show, they should be neatly covered with tape. This will make the stems easier and more pleasant to work with and will camouflage the wires, protecting them from rusting if they are to be used in mixed fresh and dry arrangements.

## USING OTHER PLANT STEMS

False stems are often helpful when dealing with very thin or fragile stems on dried material. These can be thicker, hollow stems, where the thin one is carefully pushed down the other. Or a thick stem can be taped to a thin one.

## BOWS

It is possible to make bows in a variety of ways but the simplest both to make and to use is the type which is formed from separate tails and loops. (Examples are shown in 'Helter-Skelter', 'The Christmas Story' and 'Pastel Colours'.) Each piece is made by cutting an appropriate length of ribbon for a loop or a tail. The ends are pleated in and wired round firmly, leaving a wire stem for inserting it into the arrangement. Group the various pieces to form a bow. A medium gauge wire will generally be satisfactory. (See the diagram on page 88.)

Overlapping layers, and mixing more than one shade or different widths are just some variations which can be tried.

In the same way loop effects can be made with narrow leaves such as *Phalaris arundinacea* 'Picta' (gardener's garters). Fresh or glycerine-treated leaves are the most suitable; air dried leaves tend to be very brittle.

### 'GRAPES'

The form of a bunch of grapes is an attractive addition to many flower designs and bunches of similar shape can be made from other plant material. Here are two examples.

With alder cones ('Thanksgiving Garland').
Wire each well-opened cone with a thin-gauge wire and then form into a bunch, starting with a single small cone for the tip. Grade the size a little as you work back and increase the number but do not make too large a bunch with these small, dainty cones. Twist the wires together, leaving sufficient length for fixing into the arrangement. Then trim off the surplus and neaten. If necessary, cover the wires with florist's tape. The finished bunch can be lightly sprayed with paint or glittered.

With peach stones.
This idea for a bolder bunch also comes from the designer of the Thanksgiving garland. Drill each stone with a fine drill and then wire (using a medium gauge), tape each stem and then bunch them together. Grade the stones so that the smallest will be at the tip and the largest grouped together nearest to the stem. Make a good sized bunch, then twist the stems together. Neaten but leave enough stem for fixing. Then give a spray of gold, or whatever colour suits the design.

### FLOWER FORMS

Fantasy flowers ('Ring of Welcome').
Each petal of a fantasy flower is made from two stripped honesty seedpods (*Lunaria annua*). They are sealed together with double-sided transparent adhesive tape and with a thin wire placed between the two pods. A seedhead, such as love-in-a-mist (*Nigella damascena*), or a tiny cone, is given a wire stem and this is used for the centre. Round this centre, group the petals into a flower form. Take the wires round the central stem neatly and cut all surplus away. Cover the stem with florist's tape. Curve the petals back with finger and thumb and then spray lightly with aquamarine paint and, finally, give a light spray of gold.

'Carnations' ('Ring of Welcome').
Carnation-type flowers can be made from corn-cob husks. Pull the husks off backwards in narrow strips and they will have a natural curl to them. Retain the curled part and allow these to dry thoroughly. Wire round the straight ends of the curls and group enough to form a

carnation shape. Neatly finish the stem by cutting away any surplus wire and then bind with florist's tape.

'Roses' ('Ring of Welcome').
These 'roses' are made from glycerine-preserved *Ruscus aculeatus* (butcher's broom) and *Eucalyptus gunnii* (gum tree) leaves. Each leaf is wired with fine gauge wire placed at the back and the wire held in place by adhesive tape. Leave an end of wire on each leaf. Form the flower by mixing the two kinds of leaves together; this will give interest because of the variation in shape and the slight difference in the mahogany-red colours which they take from the solution. Twist the wires into one neat stem and then tape.

Cone Flowers ('Evergreen', 'Thanksgiving Day Dinner').
Give each cone a wire stem. Cones of about 3 cm ($1\frac{1}{4}$ in) length will be about the right size. For petals, use single pieces of stripped honesty seedpods (*Lunaria annua*). To form the flowers, glue each petal in place around the fully open cone, starting at the lowest layer and working around about twice. The top of the cone becomes the centre of the flower. Trying to take petals right up to the top makes a rather too bulky finish for most arrangements.

Poinsettias ('Crimson and Gold').
These are described on page 80.

# INDEX